The Art of Distillation

An Alchemical Manuscript

Being

Certain Select Treatises

on

Alchemy and Hermetic Medicine

By

John French

The Epistle Dedicatory

To My Much Honored Friend, Tobias Garbrand, Doctor of Physick and Principal of Gloucester Hall in Oxford.

Sir ! It is my ambition to let the world know upon what score it is that I do especially honor men. It is not, Sir!, as they are highborn heirs of the great potentates, for which most honor them (and upon which account I also shall not deny them their due) but as they excell in honesty and are friends to art. That poor philosophers should take no delight in riches, and rich men should take delight in philosophy, is to me an argument, that there is more delight, honor, and satisfaction in the one than in the enjoyment of the other.

I once read of a nobleman's porter who let in all that were richly apparelled, but excluded a poor philosopher. But I should, if I had been in his place, have rather let in the philosopher, without the gay clothes, than the gay clothes without the philosopher. As long as I have sense or reason, I shall improve them to the honor of the art, especially that of alchemy. In the perfection thereof there are riches, honor, health and length of days. By it, Artefius lived 1000 years, Flamel built 28 hospitals with large revenues to them, besides churches for it, both they and diverse more were accounted philosophers, and wise men, which sounds with more honor in my ears than all the rattling and empty titles of honor whatsoever besides.

In the perfection of this art, I mean the accomplishing of the Elixir, is the sulphur of philosophers set at liberty, which gratifies the releasers thereof with three kingdoms, viz. Vegetable, Animal, and Mineral. And what cannot they do, and how honorable are they, that have the command of these? They may commend lead into gold, dying plants into fruitfulness, the sick into health, old age into youth, darkness into light, and what not? A month would fail to give you an account of their power and dominations. Now for the effecting of this I shall besides what I have advised in the Epistle to the Reader, say only this: court the mother, and you win the daughter. Prevail with nature, and the fair Diana of the philosophers is at your service.

Now, if you cannot prevail with nature for the fairest of her daughters, viz. the mercury of philosophers, yet she has other daughters of wonderful beauty also, as are the essences and magisteries of philosophers which also are endowed with riches, honor, and health, and any of these you may more easily prevail with their mother nature for. This art of alchemy is that solary art which is more noble than all the other six arts and sciences, and if it did once thoroughly shine forth out of the clouds whereby it is eclipsed, would darken all the rest (as the sun does the other six planets) or at least swallow up their light. This is that true natural philosophy which most accurately anatomizes nature and natural things, and visually demonstrates the principles and operations of them.

That empty natural philosophy which is read in the universities, is scarce the meanest hand-maid to this Queen of Arts. It is a pity that there is such great encouragement for many empty end unprofitable arts, and none for this, and such similar ingenuities which, if promoted, would render a university far more flourishing than the former. I once read or heard of a famous university beyond the sea that was fallen into decay through what cause I know not. But there was a general council held by the learned to determine how to restore it to its primitive glory. The medium at last agreed upon was the promotion of alchemy, and encouraging the artists, themselves. But I never expect to see such rational action in this nation, until shadows vanish, substances flourish, and truth prevails, which time I hope is at hand and desired by all true artists and, to my knowledge, especially by yourself, upon which account I truly honor you.

Now, to yourself therefore I crave to adumbrate something of that art which I know you will be willing, for the public good, to promote. I dedicate this treatise to you, not that it is worthy of your acceptance, but that it may receive worth by your acceptance of it. I present it to you (as men bring lead to philosophers to be tinged into gold) to receive the stamp of your favor and approbation that it may pass current, with acceptance among the sons of art, whereby you will continue to oblige him who is

Sir,

Your most obliged servant,

John French.

London,

November 25, 1650

Preface

There is a glut of chemical books, but a scarcity of chemical truths. Nature and art afford a variety of spagyrical preparations, but they are as yet partially undiscovered, partially dispersed in many books, and those of diverse languages, and partially reserved in private men's hands. When therefore I considered what need there is of, and how acceptable a general treatise on distillation might be, especially to our English nation (and the rather since Baker upon distillations is by reason of the description of a few furnaces and vessels therein, besides which there is small variety either of preparations or curiosities sold at such a high rate) I thought I could do them no better service than to present them with such a treatise of that subject which should contain in it the choicest preparations of the most select authors, both ancient and modern, and those of several languages, and which I have attained by my own long and manual experience, together with such as I have by way of exchange purchased out of the hands of private men which they had monopolized as great secrets.

But on the other hand, when I considered what a multitude of artists there is in this nation, from many of which more and better things might be expected than from myself, I was at a nonplus in my resolutions, fearing it might be accounted an unpardonable presumption in me to undertake that which might be better performed by others. But for the avoiding of this aspersion, be pleased to understand that I present not this to the world under any other notion than of a rough draft (which indeed is the work of the more unskillful and, therefore, of myself without exception) to be polished by the more expert artist.

I rejoice as at the break of day after a long and tedious night to see how this solary art of alchemy begins to shine forth out of the clouds of reproach which it has for a long time undeservedly laid under. There are two things which have eclipsed it for a long time, viz., the mists of ignorance and the specious lunary body of deceit.

Arise, O Sun of truth, and dispel these interposed fogs, that the Queen of arts may triumph in splendor! If men did believe what the art could effect, and what variety there is in it, they would be no longer straightened by, nor bound up to or lurare in verba Galeni, vel Aristotelis, but would now subscribe a new engagement to be true and faithful to the principles of Hermes and Paracelsus, as they stand established without Aristotle, their prince, and Galen and Hippocrates, their lords and masters. They would no longer stand dreaming forth, Sic dicit Galenus, but Ipse dixit Hermes. I desire not to be mistaken as if I did deny Galen his due, or Hippocrates what is his right for, indeed, they wrote excellently in many things, and deserve well thereby. That which I cannot allow of in them is their strict observation of the quadruplicity of humours (which in the school of Paracelsus and writings of Helmont, where the anatomy of humours has been most rationally and fully discussed, has been sufficiently confuted) and their confining themselves to such crude medicines which are more fit to be put into spagyrical vessels for a further digestion than into men's bodies to be fermented therein.

Certainly, if men were less ignorant, they would prefer cordial essences before crude juices, balsamical elixirs before phlegmatic waters, and mercury of philosophers before common quicksilver. But many men have so little insight in this art that they scarce believe anything beyond the distilling of waters and oil, and extracting of salts; nay, many that pretend to philosophy, and would be accounted philosophers, are so unbelieving that, as says Sendivogius, although he would have intimated the true art to them word by word, yet they would by no means understand or believe that there was any water in the philosophers sea. And, as he in this case, so I in another know diverse that will not believe that common quicksilver can of itself be turned wholly into a transparent water, or that glass can be reduced into sand and salt of which it was made, saying "fusio vitrificatoria est ultima fusio", or that an herb may be made to grow in two hours, and the idea of a plant to appear in a glass, as if the very plant itself were there, and this from the essence thereof, and such like preparations as these: the two former whereof may be done in half an hour, but the latter requiring a longer time, but yet possible. And for the possibility of the elixir, you shall as soon persuade them to believe they know nothing (which is very hard, if not an impossible thing to do) than to believe the possibility thereof. If there be any such thing (they say) why are not the possessors thereof infinitely rich, famous, doing miracles and cures and living long? These objections, especially some of them, scarce deserve an answer; yet I shall show the vanity of them and make some reply thereunto. Did not Artefius by the help of this medicine live to 1000 years? Did not Flamel build fourteen hospitals in Paris, besides as many in Boleigne, besides churches and chapels with large revenues to them all? Did not Bacon do many miracles? And Paracelsus many miraculous cures? Besides, what says Sendivogius? I have, he says, incurred more dangers and difficulties by discovering myself to have this secret than ever I had profit by it, and when I would discover myself to the great ones, it always redounded to my prejudice and danger. Can a man that carries always about him 10,000 pounds worth of jewels and gold travel everywhere up and down, safe, and not be robbed? Have not many rich money mongers been tortured into a confession where their money was concealed? Did you never hear of a vapouring fellow in London that, pretending to the knowledge of this mystery, was on a sudden caught aside by money-thirsters and by them tormented with tortures little less than those of hell, being forced thereby (if he had known it) into a discovery of it? To say nothing of being in danger of being subjected and enslaved to the pleasure of princes and of becoming instrumental to their to their luxury and tyranny, as also being deprived of all liberty, as was once Raimundus Lullius. The truth is, the greatest matter that philosophers aim at is the enjoyment of themselves, for which cause they have sequestered themselves from the world and become hermits. Well, therefore, and like a philosopher spoke Sendivogius when he said, "Believe me, if I were not a man of that state and condition that I am of, nothing would be more pleasant to me than a solitary life, or with Diogenes to live hid under a tub. For I see all things in this world to be but vanity and that deceit and covetousness prevails much, that all things are vendible, and that vice does excell virtue. I see the better things of the life to come before mine eyes and I rejoice in these. Now I do not wonder, as I did before, why philosophers, when they have attained this medicine, have not cared to have their days shortened (although by the virtue of their medicine they could have prolonged them) for every philosopher has the life to come so clearly set before his eyes, as your face is seen in a glass. Thus much by way of reply to the frivolous objections of those that believe not the verity of this art, and not only so, but will not believe it. If you should discover to them the process of the Philosopher's Stone, they would laugh at your simplicity, and I will warrant you never make use of it. Nay, if you should make projection before them, they would think that even in that there was a fallacy, so unbelieving are they. So I find them, and so I leave them, and shall forever find them the same.

There is another sort of man by whom this art has been much scandalized, and they indeed have brought a great odium upon it by carrying about, and vending their whites and reds, their sophisticated oils and salts, their dangerous and ill-prepared turbithes and aurum vitaes. And indeed it were worthwhile, and I might do good service for the nation, to discover their cheats, as their sophisticating of chemical oils with spirit of turpentine, and salts with salt extracted out of any wood-ashes and such like, but here is not place for so large a discourse as this would amount to. I shall only at this time relate to how Penotus was cheated with a sophisticated oil of gold, for he said he gave 24 ducats for the process of an aurum potabile which was much cried up and magnified at Prague, but at last it proved to be nothing but a mixture of oil of camphor, cloves, fennel-seed and of vitriol tinged with the leaves of gold. I know I shall incur the displeasure of some, but they are sophisticating, cheating mountebanks who indeed deserve to be bound to the peace, because many men, I dare swear, through their means go in danger of their lives. Better it is that their knavery should be detected, than a noble art through their villany be clouded and aspersed.

Now we must consider that there are degrees in this art, for there is the accomplishment of the elixir, itself, and there is the discovery of many excellent essences, magisteries, and spirits, etc., which abundantly recompence the discoverers thereof with profit, health, and delight. Is not Paracelsus, his Ludus that dissolves the stone and all tartarous matter in the body into a liquor, worth finding out? Is not his Tinea Scatura a most noble medicine, that extinguishes all preternatural heat in the body in a moment? Is not his alkahest a famous dissolvement that can in an instant dissolve all things into their first principles, and withall is a specificum against all distempers of the liver? Who would not take pains to make the quintessence of honey and the philosophical spirit of wine which are cordial and balsamical even to admiration? A whole day would fail to reckon up all the excellent, admirable rarities that by this spagyrical art might be brought to light, in the searching out of which, why may not the elixir, itself, at last be attained unto? Is it not possible for them that pass through many philosophical preparations to unfold at last the riddles and hieroglyphics of the philosophers? Or were they all mere phantoms? Is there no fundamentum in re for this secret? Is there no sperm in gold? Is it not possible to exalt it for multiplication? Is there no universal spirit in the world? Is it not possible to find that collected in one thing which is dispersed in all things? What is that which makes gold incorruptible? What induced the philosophers to examine gold for the matter of their medicine? Was not all gold once living? Is there none of this living gold, the matter of philosophers, to be had? Did Sendivogius, the last of known philosophers, spend it all? Surely, there is matter enough for philosophers, and also some philosophers at this day for the matter, although they are unknown to us. There are, says Sendivogius, without doubt many men of a good conscience both of high and low degree (I speak knowingly) that have this medicine and keep it secretly. if so, let no man be discouraged in the prosecution of it, especially if he takes along with him the five keys which Nollius sets down which indeed all philosophers with one consent enjoin the use and observation of.

1. Seeing it is a divine and celestial thing, it must be sought for from above, and that not without a full resolution for a pious and charitable improvement of it.

2. Before you take yourself to the work, propound to yourself what you seek, and enter not upon the practice until you are first well versed in the theory. For it is much better to learn with your brain and imagination than with your hands and costs, and especially study nature well, and see if your proposals are agreeable to the possibility thereof.

3. Diligently read the sayings of true philosophers, read them over again and again and again and meditate on them, and take heed that you do not read the writings of imposters instead of the books of the true philosophers. Compare their sayings with the possibility of nature, and obscure places clear ones, and where philosophers say they have erred, do beware, and consider well the general axioms of philosophers, and read so long until you see a sweet harmony, and consent in the sayings of them.

4. Imagine not high things, but in all things imitate nature, viz. in matter, in removing what is heterogeneous, in weight, in color, in fire, in working, in slowness of working, and let the operations not be vulgar, nor your vessels. Work diligently and constantly.

5. If it is possible, acquaint your self thoroughly with some true philosophers. Although they will not directly discover themselves that they have this secret, yet by one circumstance or another it may be concluded how near they are to it. Would not any rational man that had been conversant with Bacon, and seeing him do such miraculous things, or with Sendivogius who did intimate the art to some word by word, have concluded that they were not ignorant of it? There have been philosophers, and perhaps still are, that although they will not discover how it is made, yet may certify you, to the saving of a great deal of costs, pains, and time, how it is made. And to be convinced of an error is a great step to the truth. If Ripley had been by any tutor convinced of those many errors before he had bought his knowledge at

so dear a rate, he had long before, with less charges attained to his blessed desire.

And as a friendly tutor in this, so in all spagyrical preparations whatsoever, is of all things most necessary. A faithful well experienced master will teach you more in the mysteries of alchemy in a quarter of a year than by your own studies and chargeable operations you will learn in seven years. In the first place, therefore, and above all things apply yourself to an expert, faithful, and communicative artist, and account it a great gain if you can purchase his favor, though with a good gratuity, to lead you through the manual practice of the chiefest and choicest preparations. I said apply yourself to an artist, for there is scarce any process in all of chemistry so easy that he who never saw it done will be to seek, and commit some errors in the doing of it. I said expert that he may be able to instruct you aright; faithful, that as he is able, so may faithfully perform what he promises; and communicative, that he may be free in discovering himself and his art to you. The truth is, most artists reserve that to themselves, which they know, either out of a desire to be admired the more for their undiscovered secrets or out of envy to others' knowledge. But how far this humor is approvable in them, I leave it to others to judge; and as for my part, I have here communicated upon the account of a bare acceptance only what I have with many years of pains, much reading, and great costs known. There is but one thing which I desire to be silent in, as touching the process thereof. As for the thing itself to be prepared, what it is I have elsewhere in this treatise expressed. And the preparing of that is indeed a thing worth of anyone's knowing, and which perhaps hereafter I may make known to some. I am of the same mind with Sendivogius that the fourth monarchy which is northern is dawning, in which (as the ancient philosophers did divine) all arts and sciences shall flourish, and greater and more things shall be discovered than in the three former. These monarchies the philosophers reckon not according to the more potent, but according to the corners of the world, whereof the northern is the last and, indeed, is no other than the Golden Age in which all tyranny, oppression, envy, and covetousness shall cease, when there shall be one prince and one people abounding with love and mercy, and flourishing in peace, which day I earnestly expect.

In the meantime, if what I know may add to your experience, you may have it freely. And if I shall see that this treatise of distillation passes with acceptance among the artists of this nation, I shall hereafter gratify them for their good will with two other parts of chemistry, viz. sublimation and calcination. And I hope this will be occasion to set the more expert artist on work, for the communicating their experiences to the world. One thing (courteous reader) let me desire you to take notice of, viz. whereas every process is set down plain, yet all of them must be proceeded in secundum artem alchymistae (which art indeed is obtained by experience) and therefore many that work according to the bare process effect not what they intend, and the reason is this, because there was some art of the alchemist wanting. To conclude, if you know more or better things than these, be candid and impart them (considering that I wrote these for them that know them not); if not, accept the endeavors of your friend,

John French.

BOOK I

WHAT DISTILLATION IS AND THE KINDS THEREOF

I shall not stand here to show where the art of distillation had its origin, as being a thing not easily to be proved and, if known, yet little conducing to our ensuing discourse. But let us understand what distillation is, of which there are three principal and chief definitions or descriptions:

1. Distillation is a certain art of extracting the liquor, or the humid part of things by virtue of heat (as the matter shall require) being first resolved into a vapor and then condensed again by cold.
2. Distillation is the art of extracting the spiritual and essential humidity from the phlegmatic, or of the phlegmatic from the spiritual.
3. Distillation is the changing of gross thick bodies into a thinner and liquid substance, or separation of the pure liquor from the impure feces.

I shall treat of distillation according to all these three acceptions, and no otherwise, hence I shall exclude sublimation and degrees of heat there are, and which are convenient for every operation, and they are principally four.

The first in only a warmth, as is that of horse dung, of the sun, of warm water, and the vapor thereof, which kind of heat serves for putrefaction and digestion.

The second is of seething water and the vapor thereof, as also of ashes, and serves to distill those things which are subtle and moist, as also for the rectifying of any spirit or oil.

The third is of sand and filings of iron which serves to distill things subtle and dry, or gross and moist.

The fourth is of a naked fire - close, open or with a blast which serves to distill metals and minerals and hard gummy things, such as amber, etc. I do not say serves only to distill these, for many former distillations are performed by this heat, as the distilling of spirits and oils, etc., in a copper still over a naked fire; but these may be distilled by the two former degrees of heat. But minerals and such like cannot but by this fourth degree alone.

OF THE MATTER AND FORM OF FURNACES

The matter of furnaces is various, for they may be made either of brick and clay, or clay alone with whites of eggs, hair and filings or iron (and of these if the clay be fat are made the best and most durable furnaces) or of iron or copper, cast or forged. The forms also of furnaces are various.

The fittest form for distillation is round; for so the heat of the fire being carried up equally diffuses itself every way, which happens not in a furnace of another figure, as four square or triangular, for the corners disperse and separate the force of the fire. Their magnitude must be such as shall be fit for the receiving of the vessel; their thickness so great as necessity shall seem to require; only thus much observe, that if they be of forged iron or copper, they must be coated inside, especially if you intend to use them for a strong fire. They must be made with two bottoms distinguished, as it were, into two forges, the one below which may receive the ashes, the other above to contain the fire. The bottom of this upper must either be an iron grate or else an iron plate perforated with many holes so that the ashes may the more easily fall down into the bottom, which otherwise would put out the fire. Yet some furnaces have three partitions, as the furnace for reverberation, and the register furnace. In the first and lowest the ashes are received. In the second the fire is put, and in the third of the furnace for reverberation, the matter which is to be reverberated. This third ought to have a semi-circular cover so that the heat may be reflected upon the contained matter. The bottom of the third and uppermost partition of the register furnace must be either a plate of iron or a smooth stone perforated with holes, having stopples of stone fitted thereunto which you may take out or put in, as you would have the heat increased or decreased. In the top or upper part of all these furnaces where it shall seem most fit, there must be two or three holes made, that by them the smoke may more freely pass out and the air let in to make the fire burn stronger if need requires, or else which are to be shut with stopples made fit to them. The mouths of the fore-mentioned partitions must have shutters, just like an oven's mouth, with which you may shut them closed or leave them open if you would have the fire burn stronger. But in defect of a furnace or fit matter to make one, we may use a kettle or a pot set upon a trivet, as we shall show when we come to give you a description of the furnace and vessels. The truth of the matter is, a good artist will make any still, yea and in half a day's time make a furnace or something equivalent to it for any operations.

OF VESSELS FIT FOR DISTILLATION

Vessels for distillation are of various matter and form. For they may be either of lead, which I altogether disapprove of for that they turn the liquors into a white and milky substance besides the malignity they give to them, or they may be of copper, iron, or tin which are better than the former. They may be of jug-metal, or potter's metal glazed, or glass which are the best of all, where they may be used without fear of breaking or melting. Some make them of silver, but they are very changeable. They that are able and willing may have the benefit of them.

OF LUTES FOR COATING OF GLASSES AND FOR CLOSURES AS ALSO SEVERAL WAYS OF STOPPING GLASSES

The best lute is made thus. Take of loam and sand tempered with salt water (which keeps it from cleaving). To these add the caput mortuary of vitriol or aqua fortis, and scalings of iron, and temper them well together. This serves to coat retorts or any glass vessels that must endure a most strong fire, and will never fail if well made. Some add flax, beaten glass, and pots and flints, etc.
Take unslaked lime and linseed oil. Mix them well together and make thereof a lute which will be so hard that no spirit will pierce it, and this serves for the closure of glasses.
Or, moisten an ox bladder in the white of an egg beaten to water, or in defect of a bladder, use paper and bind them round where the vessels are joined together, one over another two or three times.
Or, if the spirits in the glass be exceedingly corrosive, then use the caput mortuary of aqua fortis, linseed oil, and chalk mixed together.
If a glass be cracked, then wet a linen cloth in the white of an egg beaten to water, and lay upon it, an upon that presently while it is wet, sift some unslaked lime and press it close with your hand. When that is dry, lay on another cloth thus wet as before and on it sift more lime.
A vessel may be stopped so close with quicksilver that no spirit can breathe forth, by which means the glass will be preserved from breaking

by the enclosed spirits (for the head will first yield before the glass breaks). The vessel must be made as the figure hereunder shows. This also is a good way to preserve spirits already distilled from the air.

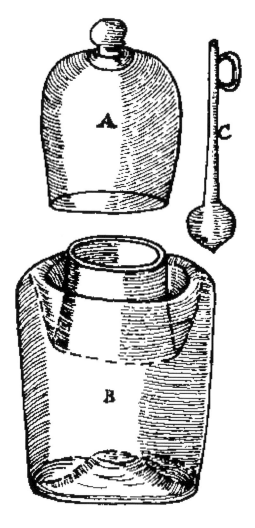

A. Signifies the head or cover.

B. The body or vessel itself.

C. The little glass to take out the liquor that is in the vessel because it cannot well be poured out, as by reason of the quicksilver which will be apt to be lost, so by reason of the form of the vessel itself.

D . A false bottom where the quicksilver must lie, into which the head must be set upon the quicksilver so that the quicksilver may come above the bottom of the head.

Also, you may make stopples of glasses ground so smooth that no vapor can get forth by them, as you may see by this pattern.

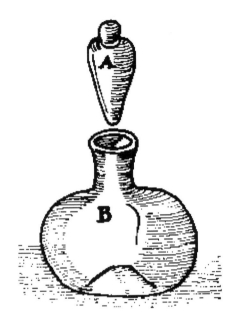

A. Signifies the stopple of glass ground very smooth and fit to the mouth of the vessel.
B. The glass body.

But the best way is to have a crooked pipe which may have quicksilver in it, and be well luted to the body that no spirit can get forth. By this means the glass will never break, for the quicksilver will first yield.

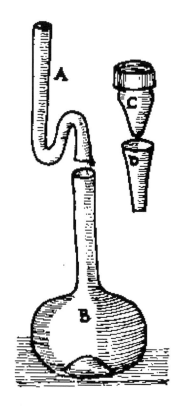

A. The crooked pipe.
B. The glass body.

Or upon the top of a glass stopple there may be fastened some lead, that if the spirit be too strong, it will only heave up the stopple and let it fall down again.

C. The glass stopple with lead on the top.
D. The mouth of the vessel itself.

Now the way to nip up a glass, or seal it up hermetically is after this manner .

Put what matter you please into a bolt head with a long neck or pipe, put this pipe through a pan that has a little hole made in the bottom, that the top of it may be three or four inches above the pan. Close up the hole round about the pipe with clay. Then put coals in the pan and kindle first those that are furtherest off from the pipe that the heat may come by degrees to the pipe (for otherwise a sudden heat will break it). When the pipe is hot, blow the coals about it until it melts. Then with a pair of shears, cut it off where it is melted, and then with a pair of tongs close it together.

Note that after you have closed it you must put the burning coals upon the top thereof, and let it thus stand until all be cold which must be done by degrees, for otherwise the glass will certainly crack in the place where it is nipped.

Note that the pan must stand upon some frame or some hollow place that there may be a passage for the pipe to come through it. Also the bolt head must stand upon a trivet or some other firm place according to this figure.

AN EXPLANATION OF SUCH HARD WORDS AND TERMS OF ART WHICH ARE USED IN THIS ENSUING TREATISE

AMALGAMATION is a calcining or corroding of metals with quicksilver, and it is done thus. Take any metal except iron, beaten into thin leaves or very small powder. Mix it with about eight parts of quicksilver (which may the better be done if both be heated first) that they may become one uniform mass. Evaporate the quicksilver over the fire, and the metal will be left in the bottom as a thin calx.

CALCINATION is the reducing of anything into a calx, and making it friable, and it may be done two ways - by firing, either by reducing into ashes or by reverberating; or by corrosion, either by amalgamation, precipitation, fumigation or vaporation, cementation or stratification.

CIRCULATION is when any liquor is so placed in digestion that it shall rise up and fall down, rise up and fall down, and so do continually, and thereby become more digested and mature, for which use for the most part we use a pelican.

CLARIFICATION is the separation of the gross feces from any decoction or juice, and it is done three ways - by the white of an egg, by digestion, or by filtration.

COAGULATION is the reducing of any liquid thing to a thicker substance by evaporating the humidity.

COHOBATION is the frequent abstraction of any liquor, poured often on the feces from whence it was distilled, by distillation.

CONGELATION is when any liquor being decocted to the heights is afterwards, by settling into any cold place, turned into a transparent substance like unto ice.

CORROSION is the calcining of bodies by corrosive things.

DECANTATION is the pouring off of any liquor which has a settling by inclination.

DELIQUIUM is the dissolving of a hard body into a liquor, as salt, or the powder of any calcined matter, etc., in a moist place.

DESCENSION is when the essential juice dissolved from the matter to be distilled does descend or fall downward.

DESTUMATION is the taking off the froth that floats on the top with a spoon or feather, or by percolation.

DISTILLATION is the extracting of the humid part of things by virtue of heat, being first resolved into a vapor, and then condensed again by cold. Thus it is generally taken, but how more particularly, I shall afterward show.

DIGESTION is a concocting or maturation of crude things by an easy and gentle heat.

DISSOLUTION is the turning of bodies into a liquor by the addition of some humidity.

DULCORATION or culcification is either the washing off of the salt from any matter that was calcined therewith, with warm water, in which the salt is dissolved and the matter dulcified. Or it is the sweetening of things with sugar, or honey, or syrup.

ELEVATION is the rising of any matter in matter of fume or vapor by virtue of heat.

EVAPORATION or EXHALATION is the vaporing away of any moisture.

EXALTATION is when any matter does by digestion attain to a greater purity.

EXPRESSION is the extracting of any liquor by the hand or by a press.

EXTRACTION is the drawing forth of an essence from a corporeal matter by some fit liquor as spirit of wine, the feces remaining in the bottom.

FERMENTATION is when anything is resolved into itself, and is rarified and ripened, whether it be done by any ferment added to it or by digestion only.

FILTRATION is the separation of any liquid matter from its feces by making it run through a brown paper made like a tunnel, or a little bag of woolen cloth, or through shreds.

FIXATION is the making of any volatile spiritual body endure the fire and not fly away, whether it be done by often reiterated distillations, or sublimations, or by the adding of some fixing thing to it.

FUMIGATION is the calcining of bodies by the fume of sharp spirits, whether vegetable or mineral, the bodies being laid over the mouth of the vessel wherein the sharp spirit s are .

HUMECTATION or irrigation is a sprinkling of moisture upon anything.

IMBIBITION is when any dry body drinks in any moisture that is put upon it.

IMPREGNATION is when any dry body has drunk in so much moisture that it will admit of no more.

INCORPORATION is a mixing of a dry and moist body together so as to make a uniform mass of them.

INFUSION is the putting of any hard matter into liquor, for the virtue thereof to be extracted.

INSOLATION is digestion of things in the sun.

LEVIGATION is the reducing of any hard matter into a most fine powder.

LIQUATION is a melting or making anything fluid.

LUTATION is either the stoppings of the orifices of vessels so that no vapor passes out, or the coating of any vessel to preserve it from breaking in the fire.

MACERATION is the same as digestion.

MATURATION is the exalting of a substance that is immature, and crude to be ripened and concocted.

MENSTRUUM is any liquor that serves for the extracting of the essence of anything.

PRECIPITATION is when bodies corroded by corrosive spirits either by the evaporating of the spirits remain in the bottom, or by pouring something upon the spirit, as oil of tartar, or a good quantity of water, do fall to the bottom.

PURIFICATION is a separation of any liquor from its feces whether it be done by clarification, filtration, or digestion.

PUTREFACTION is the resolution of a mixed body into itself by natural gentle heat.

QUINTESSENCE is an absolute, pure, and well digested medicine drawn from any substance, either animal, vegetable, or mineral.

RECTIFICATION is either the drawing of the phlegm from the spirit or of the spirit from the phlegm, or the exaltation of any liquor by a reiterated distillation.

REVERBERATION is the reducing of bodies into a calx by a reflecting flame.

SOLUTION is a dissolving or attenuating of bodies.

STRATIFICATION is a strewing of corroding powder on plates of metal by course.

SUBLIMATION is an elevating or raising of the matter to the upper part of the vessel by way of a subtle powder.

SUBTILIATION is the turning of a body into a liquor or into a fine powder.

TRANSMUTATION is the changing of a thing in substance, color, and quality.

VOLATILE is that which flyeth the fire.

RULES TO BE CONSIDERED IN DISTILLATION

I

Make choice of a fit place in your house for the furnace, so that it may neither hinder anything, nor be in danger of the falling of anything into it that shall lie over it. For a forcing furnace, it will be best to set it in a chimney, because a strong heat is used to it, and many times there are used brands which will smoke, and the fire being great, the danger thereof may be prevented and of things of a malign and venerate quality being distilled in such a furnace, the fume or vapor, if the glass should break may be carried up into the chimney which otherwise will fly about the room to thy prejudice.

2

In all kinds of distillation the vessels are not to be filled too full, for if you distill liquors they will run over, and if other more solid things the one part will be burned before the other part be at all worked upon. But fill the fourth part of gourds, the half of retorts, the third part of copper vessels, and in rectifying of spirits fill the vessel half full.

3

Let those things which are flatulent, as wax, resin, and such like, as also those things which do easily boil up, as honey, be put in a lesser quantity and be distilled in greater vessels with the addition of salt, sand, or such like.

4

There be some things which require a strong fire, yet you must have a care that the fire not be too vehement, for fear their nature should be destroyed.

5

You must have a care that the lute with which vessels are closed do not give vent and alter the nature of the liquor, especially when a strong fire is to be used.

6

Acid liquors have this peculiar property, that the weaker part goes forth first and the stronger last. But in fermented and liquors the spirit goes first, then the phlegm.

7

If the liquor retains a certain empyreuma or smatch of the fire, you shall help it by putting it into a glass close stopped and so exposing it to the heat of the sun, and now and then opening the glass that the fiery impression may exhale. Or else let the glass stand in a cold moist place.

8

When you put water into a seething Balneum wherein there are glasses, let it be hot or else you will endanger breaking the glasses.

9

When you take any earthen or glass vessel from the fire, expose it not to the cold air too suddenly, for fear it should break.

10

If you would have a Balneum as hot as ashes, put sand or sawdust into it, that the heat of the water may be therewith kept in and made more intense.

11

If you would make a heat with horse dung, the manner is this, viz., make a hole in the ground. Then lay one course of horse dung a foot thick, then a course of unslaked lime a foot thick, and then another of dung, as before. Then set in your vessel, and lay around it lime and horse dung mixed together. Press it down very hard. You must sprinkle it every other day with water. When it ceases to be hot, then take it out and put in more.

12

Note that always sand or ashes must be well sifted, for otherwise a coal or stone therein may break your glass.

13

The time for putrefaction of things is various, for if the thing to be putrefied is vegetable and green, less time is required; if dry, a longer time is required. Minerals require the longest of all. Thus much note, that things are sooner putrefied in cloudy weather than in fair.

14

If you would keep vegetables fresh and green all year, gather them on a dry day and put them into an earthen vessel which you must stop close and set in a cold place and, as Glauberus says, they will keep fresh a whole year .

15

Do not expect to extract the essence of any vegetable unless by making use of the feces, left after distillation; for if you take those feces, as for example of a nettle, and make a decoction thereof and strain it and set it in the frost, it will be congealed and in it will appear a thousand leaves of nettles with their prickles which when the decoction is again resolved by heat, vanish away, which shows that the essence of the vegetables lies in the salt thereof.

16

In all your operations, diligently observe the processes which you read and vary not a little from them, for sometimes a small mistake or neglect spoils the whole operation and frustrates your expectations.

17

Try not at first experiments of great cost or great difficulty, for it will be a great discouragement to you, and you will be very apt to mistake.

18

If any would enter upon the practice of chemistry, let him apply himself to some expert artist for to be instructed in the manual operation of things, for by this means he will learn more in two months than he can by his practice and study in 7 years, as also avoid much pains and cost and redeem much time which else of necessity he will lose.

19

Enter not upon any operation unless it be consistent with the possibility of nature which, therefore, you must endeavor as much as possible to understand well.

20

Do not interpret all things you read according to the literal sense, for philosophers when they wrote anything too excellent for the vulgar to know, expressed it enigmatically that the sons of Art only might understand it

21

In all your operations propose a good end to yourself, as not to use any excellent experiment that you shall discover to any ill end, but for the public good.

22

It will be necessary that you know all such instruments that you shall use about your furnace and glasses, whereof some are already expressed and some more are shown in the following pages.

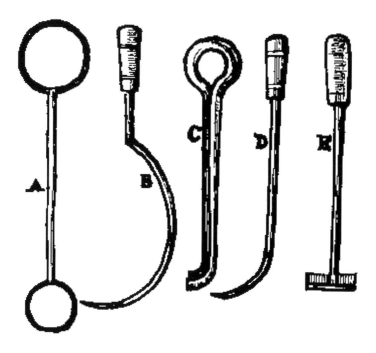

A. Signifies an iron rod with two rings at the ends thereof, which must be heated red hot and applied to that part of the glass which you would break off. When you have held it there so long until the glass becomes very hot, then take it off and drop some cold water where you would have it break off, and it will presently crack in sunder. These rings are for such glasses as will go into them. You must have diverse of this sort, even of all sizes.

B. An iron hook which must be heated hot and applied to any great glass that will not go into a ring. This hook has a wooden handle.

C. A pair of tongs which are for diverse uses.

D. A crooked iron to rake between the grates to clear them.

E. An iron rake to rake the ashes out of the ash-hole.

A thread dipped in melted brimstone and tied about a glass and then fired may serve instead of the iron rings and the hook.

COMMON DISTILLED SIMPLE WATERS ARE MADE THUS

Take what herbs or flowers you please and put them into a common cold still and let them distill gently.

This is the form of a common cold still.

But note that this kind of water is but the phlegm of the vegetable which you distill and has very little virtue or odor in it. Only roses and mints and two or three more have an odor, but all besides have as little virtue as common distilled water.
I do not deny but that it may be so ordered that these kinds of waters may partake both of the smell and strength of their vegetables in a good measure, and it is thus.

TO MAKE WATERS IN A COLD STILL THAT SHALL HAVE THE FULL SMELL AND VIRTUE OF THE VEGETABLE

Take what herbs, flowers, or roots you please (so that they be green). Bruise them and mix with them some leaven, and let them stand close covered for four or five days. Then distill them after the manner aforesaid.

ANOTHER WAY TO MAKE WATER TASTE AND SMELL STRONGLY OF ITS VEGETABLE

When you have distilled any vegetable in a cold still after the usual manner (so that you take heed you dry not the herb too much, which you may prevent by putting a brown paper in the bottom of the still, giving it a gentle fire and turning the cake before it is quite dried) take the cakes that remain in the bottom of the still and the water that is distilled from thence (having a good quantity thereof) and put them into a hot still and let them stand warm for the space of 24 hours, and then distill them. Then if you would have the water strong, put the said water into more fresh cakes, casting away the other and do as before. This is the truest and best way to have the water of any vegetable. Also, you shall by this way purchase some oil which is to be separated and to be kept by itself.

TO MAKE WATER AT ANY TIME OF THE YEAR IN A COLD STILL WITHOUT GREEN HERBS, SO THAT THE WATER SHALL SMELL STRONG OF THE HERB

Put fair water into the body of the cold still. Then hang a bag full of that herb that you would have the water of, being first dried, or seed or root thereof first bruised, and then make a strong fire under the still. Note that those vegetables of which the water is made after this and the former manner must be of a fragrant smell, for such as have but little or no smell cannot yield a water of any considerable odor.

ANOTHER WAY TO MAKE A WATER TASTE AND SMELL STRONG OF ITS VEGETABLES

Take of the dry herb, or seed or root bruised, to a pound of each put 12 pints of spring water. Distill them in a hot still or alembick, and the water that is distilled off put upon more of the fresh herbs, seeds, or roots. Do this three or four times and you shall have a water full of the virtue of the vegetable, being almost as strong as a spirit.

TO MAKE THE WATER OF THE FLOWERS OF JASMINE, HONEYSUCKLES OR WOODBINE, VIOLETS, LILIES, ETC. RETAIN THE SMELL OF THEIR FLOWERS

The reason why these flowers in the common way of distillation yield a water of no fragrancy at all, although they themselves are very odoriferous, are either because if a stronger fire be made in the distilling of them the grosser and more earthy spirit comes out with the finer, and troubles it, as it is in case the flowers be crushed or bruised (where the odor upon the same account is lost) or because the odoriferous spirit thereof being thin and very subtle rises with a gentle heat, but for lack of body vapors away. The art therefore that is here required is to prevent the mixing of the grosser spirit with the finer and to give such a body to the finer that shall not embase it, and it is thus:

Take either of the aforesaid flowers gathered fresh, and at noon in a fair day, and let them not at all be bruised. Infuse a handful of them in two quarts of white wine (which must be very good or else you labor in vain) for the space of half an hour. Then take them forth and infuse in the same wine the same quantity of fresh flowers. This do eight or ten times, but still remember that they be not infused above half an hour. For according to the rule of infusion, a short stay of the body that has a fine spirit, in the liquor receives the spirit; but a longer stay confounds it, because it draws forth the earthy part withall which destroys the finer. Then distill this liquor (all the flowers being first taken out) in a glass gourd in a very gentle Balneum, or over a vapor of hot water, the joints of the glass being very well closed, and you shall have a water of a most fragrant odor. By this means the spirit of the wine which serves to body the fine odoriferous spirit of the flowers arises as soon as the fine spirit, itself, without any earthiness mixed with it.

Note that in defect of wine, aqua vitae will serve; also strong beer, but not altogether so well, because there is more gross earthiness in it than in wine.

The water of either of these flowers is a most fragrant perfume and may be used as a very delicate sweet water, and is no small secret.

A. Shows the head of the alembic.

B. The body thereof placed in a brass vessel made for that purpose.

C. A brass vessel perforated in many places to receive the vapor of the water. This vessel shall contain the alembic compassed about with sawdust, not only that it may better and longer retain the heat of the vapor, but also lest it should be broken by the hard touch of the brass vessel.

D. Shows the brass vessel containing the water as it is placed in the furnace.

E. The furnace containing the vessel.

F. A funnel by which you may now and then pour in water to replace what is vanished and dissipated by the heat of the fire.

G. The receiver.

The delineation of a Balneum Mariae may also serve to distill with ashes.

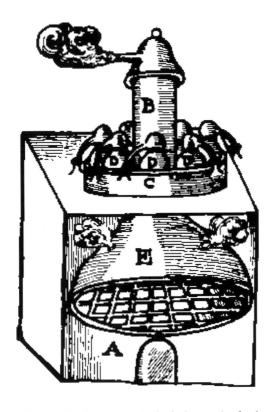

A. Shows the furnace with the hole to take forthe the ashes.

B. Shows another furnace, as it were set in the other. Now it is of brass and runs through the middle of the kettle made also of brass, so that the contained water or ashes may be the more easily heated.

C. The kettle wherein the water, ashes, or sand are contained.

D. The alembic set in the water, ashes, or sand with the mouths of the receivers.

E. The bottom of the second brass furnace, whose top is marked with "B", which contains the fire.

A WATER OUT OF BERRIES IS MADE THUS

Take of what berries you please, being full ripe. Put them into a gourd glass, strewing upon them a good quantity of powdered sugar. Cover them close and let them stand three weeks or a month. Then distill them in Balneum .

After this manner strawberries, raspberries, elderberries, and black cherries may be distilled. But note that such as have stones must first be bruised together with their stones .

A SWEATING WATER MADE OF ELDERBERRIES

Take of elderberries as many as you please. Press out the juice thereof, and to every gallon put a pint of white wine vinegar, of the lees of white wine a pint. Let them stand in a wooden vessel which you must then set in some warm place near the fireside for the space of a week. Then distill them in a hot still or alembic.

The furnace for a Balneum Mariae with the alembics and their receivers.

A. Shows the brass kettle full of water.

B. The cover of the kettle perforated in two places, to give passage forth to the ve s s els .

A pipe or chimney added to the kettle, wherein the fire is contained to heat the water.

D. The alembic consisting of its body and head.

E. The receiver whereinto the distilled liquor runs.

The effigies of another Balneum Mariae not so easy to be removed as the former .

A. Shows the vessel or copper that contains the water.

B. The alembic set in water.

But lest the bottom of the alembic being half full should float up and down in the water, and so strike against the sides of the kettle, I have thought good to show you the way and means to prevent that danger.

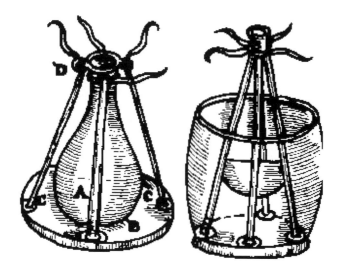

A. Shows the vessel or glass alembic .
B. A plate of lead whereon it stands.
C. Strings that bind the alembic to the plate.
D. Rings through which the strings are put to fasten the alembic.

In defect of a furnace for a Balneum, you may make use of a pot set upon a trivet after this manner.

An ounce or two of this water of elderberries is a very excellent sudorific, and is very good in all diseases that require sweat, as also in hydropical diseases.

WATER OUT OF ROTTEN APPLES IS MADE THUS

Take as many rotten apples as you please. Bruise and distill them either in a common cold still or gourd glasses in Balneum.

This water is of greater use in fevers and hot distempers than the common distilled waters of any cold vegetables.

It is very good in any hot distemper of the veins and sharpness of the urine .

It is very good in the inflammations of the eyes.

HOW TO MAKE AQUA VITAE AND SPIRIT OF WINE OUT OF WINE

Take of what wine you please. Put it into a copper still, two parts of three being empty. Distill it with a worm until no more spirit comes off. Then this spirit will serve for the making of any spirits out of vegetables, but if you would have it stronger, distill it again and half will remain behind as an insipid phlegm. And if you would have it yet stronger, distill it again, for every distillation will leave behind one moity of phlegm or thereabouts. So shall you have a most pure and strong spirit of wine.

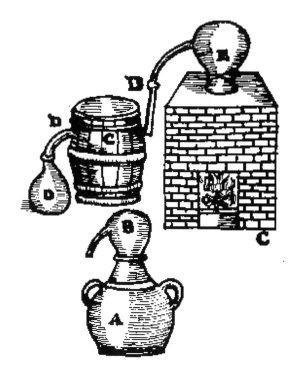

A. Shows the bottom which ought to be of copper.

B. The head.

C. The barrel filled with cold water to refrigerate and condense the water and oil that run through the pipe or worm that is put through it.

D. A pipe of brass or pewter, or rather a worm of tin running through the barrel.

E. The alembic set in the furnace with the fire under it.

HOW TO MAKE AQUA VITAE OUT OF BEER

Take the stale strong beer or rather the grounds thereof and put it into a copper still with a worm. Distill it gently (or otherwise it will make the head of the still fly up) and there will come forth a weak spirit, which is called low wine, of which when you have a good quantity you may distill it again of itself, and there will come forth a good aqua vitae.

And if you distill it two or three times more, you shall have as strong a spirit as out of wine and, indeed, between which and the spirit of wine you shall perceive none or very little difference.

HOW TO RECTIFY SPIRIT OF WINE OR AQUA VITAE

Distill it in Balneum until the last drop that comes off be hot and full of spirit .
Note that every time there will remain in the bottom a quantity as weak as water .
Note also that every time you distill it, when you perceive that a very weak water comes over, you shall then end that distillation.

TO MAKE THE MAGISTERY OF WINE WHICH WILL BE ONE OF THE GREATEST CORDIALS AND MOST ODORIFEROUS LIQUOR IN THE WORLD

Take good old rich canary wine, put it into a glass vessel that it may fill the third part thereof, and nip it up and set it in a continual heat of horse dung for the space of four months. Then in frosty weather set it forth into the coldest place of the air you can for the space of a month that it may be congealed. And so the cold will drive in the true spirit of the wine into the center thereof and separate it perfectly from its phlegm. That which is congealed cast away. But that which is not congealed esteem as the true spirit of wine. Circulate this in a pelican with a moderate heat for the space of a month, and you will have the true magistery or spirit of wine which, as it is most cordial, so also most balsamical, exceeding all balsams for the cure of wounds.

The form of a Pelican.

The matter must be put in at the top which afterwards must be closed up.

TO MAKE ANOTHER MAGISTERY OF WINE THAT A FEW DROPS THEREOF SHALL TURN WATER INTO PERFECT WINE

Take the best canary wine as much as you please, let is stand in putrefaction forty days, then distill it in Balneum and there will come forth a spirit, and at last an oil. Separate the one from the other and rectify the spirit. Set the oil again in putrefaction forty days and then distill it. The feces that are left after the first distillation will yield a volatile salt which must be extracted without calcination, with the phlegm of the spirit. purify it well, then impregnate the salt with its spirit, and digest them. Then add the oil and digest them together until they become a red powder, which you may use as it is, or else set it in a cellar until it be dissolved into a liquor, and a few drops thereof will do as abovesaid.

TO MAKE AN OIL OF WINE

Take weak spirit of wine and distill it in a vessel of a long neck. Then pour on this spirit again upon the phlegm, and distill it again. Do this several times and you shall see the oil of the wine swim on the phlegm, which phlegm you must separate from the oil by a tunnel.
If this oil be afterward circulated for a month, it will thereby become

most odoriferous, and of a singular virtue, and good being both very cordial and balsamical.

TO EXTRACT THE SPIRIT OUT OF WINE BY THE SPIRIT OF WINE

Put spirit of wine well rectified upon Canary or Rhenish wine, so cautiously that it may not mix with, but swim upon the wine. Let them stand without stirring for the space of 48 hours. Then will the spirit that is in the wine rise up and join itself to the spirit that swims on the top, which you shall perceive by the weakness of the phlegm, and which you must let run out at a tap. This must be made in the bottom of the vessel for that purpose, and so be separated from the spirit.

TO MAKE A VERY SUBTLE SPIRIT OF WINE AT THE FIRST DISTILLING

Take white or wheaten bread as soon as it comes forth from the oven, break it in the middle, the upper side from the lower side, and hang it hot in a glass vessel over canary wine, but so that it touches not the wine. Then cover the vessel and let it so stand until the bread swells and is sufficiently impregnated with the spirit of wine which it will attract from the wine. Then take out that bread and put in more until you have a considerable quantity of bread thus moistened. Then put this bread into a glass body, distill it in Balneum, and you shall have a very subtle spirit which you may yet rectify by circulation.

By furnaces and vessels made after this insuing figure may be made four rectifications of any spirit at once.

These vessels may either stand in ashes or in Balneum.

The manner of distilling in wooden vessels.

A. Signifies the vessel wherein the copper vessel lies.
B. The copper vessel, part of which is in the furnace and part is in the vessel of wood.
C The vessel of wood wherein the matter must be that is distilled.
D The cooling vessel with the worm.
E. The receiver.
F. The trivet whereon the vessel stands.

Note that the greater the copper vessel is, and the less the wooden one is, the sooner will the liquor boil.

This furnace shows how to draw forth spirits and waters out of vegetables and animals with little cost and short time.

A balneum and a boiling vessel made of wood.

Note that on the right hand these vessels have a copper vessel hanging forth which must be set into a furnace as is above shown. And on the left hand is a cock or tap to let out the water.

The vessel on the left hand is for a balneum. The holes in the cover thereof are either to set in vessels over the fume of the water or for the necks of the glasses set in the balneum to pass through.

The vessel on your right hand is to boil water in for any use, also to brew in.

THE SPIRIT OF ANY VEGETABLE IS MADE THUS

Take of what vegetable you please, two pounds, macerate it in six gallons of aqua vitae or low wines, or sack, for the space of 24 hours. Then let them be distilled by an alembic, or hot still, putting to every pound of the spirit two ounces of most pure sugar.

Note that the two first pints may be called the stronger spirit, and the rest the weaker spirit or, indeed, the water. But if they be both mixed together, they will make an excellent middling spirit, for the former has more of the spirit of wine, and the latter more of the virtue and odor of the vegetable.

After this manner may be made the spirit of herbs, flowers, roots of vegetables, the seeds of vegetables, berries, barks, rinds, and spices. Note that the herbs and flowers must be cut small, and bruised. If you would make it stronger, then take all the foresaid spirit and as much more sack or low wines and put them upon the same quantity of fresh vegetables and distill them. Repeat this three or four times if you please

Note also that the vegetable must be dried, because else the spirit will not be so good, as if otherwise.

The form of an alembic.

A. Signifies the vessel which must be of copper, in which the matter is contained, and which must be set over a naked fire.

B. Signifies the belly that is fastened to the neck, that the neck may the more commodiously be applied to the large mouth of the vessel. But it may be so ordered that the mouth of the upper vessel and lower vessel may be so fitted that they shall not need this belly.

C. The long neck of the upper vessel where by the spirit or water is somewhat cooled.

D. The head.

E. The vessel that compasses the head into which cold water is continually poured after the heating.

F. The long receiver.

G. The top or cock letting out the water when it is hot.

THE SPIRIT OF ANY VEGETABLE MAY SUDDENLY AT ANY TIME OF THE YEAR BE MADE THUS

Take of what herb, flower, seeds, or roots you please. Fill the head of the still therewith and then cover the mouth thereof with a coarse canvas and set it on the still, having first put into it sack or low wines. Then give it fire.

If at any time you would have the spirit be of the color of its vegetable, then put of the flowers thereof dried a good quantity in the nose of the still.

TO MAKE ANY VEGETABLE YIELD ITS SPIRIT QUICKLY

Take of what vegetables you please, whether it be the seed, flower, root, fruit, or leaves thereof. Cut or bruise them small and then put them into warm water. Put yeast or berm to them, and cover them warm and let them work three days, as does beer. Then distill them and they will yield their spirit easily.

TO REDUCE THE WHOLE HERB INTO A LIQUOR WHICH MAY WELL BE CALLED THE ESSENCE THEREOF

Take the whole herb with flowers and roots and make it very clean. Then bruise it in a stone mortar and put it into a large glass vessel so two parts of three may be empty. Cover it exceeding close and let it stand in putrefaction in a moderate heat the space of half a year, and it will all be turned into a water.

TO MAKE AN ESSENCE OF ANY HERB, WHICH BEING PUT INTO A GLASS AND HELD OVER A GENTLE FIRE, THE LIVELY FORM AND IDEA OF THE HERB WILL APPEAR IN THE GLASS

Take the foregoing water and distill it in a gourd glass (the joints being well closed) in ashes, and there will come forth a water and an oil and in the upper part of the vessel will hang a volatile salt. Separate the oil from the water and keep it by itself. With the water purify the volatile salt by dissolving, filtering, and coagulating. The salt being thus purified, imbibe with the said oil until it will imbibe no more. Digest them well together for a month in a vessel hermetically sealed. And by this means you shall have a most subtle essence, which being held over a gentle heat will fly up into the glass and represent the perfect idea of that vegetable whereof it is the essence.

THE TRUE ESSENCE OR RATHER QUINTESSENCE OF ANY HERB IS MADE THUS

When you have made the water and oil of any vegetable first calcine or burn to ashes the remainder of the herb. With the ashes make a lye by pouring its own water thereon. When you have drawn out all the strength of the ashes, then take all the lye, being first filtered, and vapor it away and at the bottom you shall find a black salt which you must take and put into a crucible and melt it in a strong fire (covering the crucible all the time it is melting). After it is melted let it boil half an hour or more. Then take it out and beat it small and set it in a cellar on a marble stone or in a broad glass and it will all be resolved into a liquor. This liquor filter and vapor away the humidity until it be very dry and as white as snow. Then let this salt imbibe as much of the oil of the same vegetable as it can, but no more, lest you labor in vain. Then digest them together until the oil will not rise from the salt, but both become a fixed powder melting with an easy heat.

TO EXTRACT THE QUINTESSENCE OF ALL VEGETABLES

Take of what spices, flowers, seeds, herbs, woods you please and put them into rectified spirit of wine. Let the spirit extract in digestion until no more feces fall to the bottom but all their essence is gone into the spirit of wine. Upon being thus impregnated, pour a strong spirit of salt and digest it in Balneum until an oil swims above which separate with a tunnel or draw of the spirit of wine in balneum. The oil will remain clear at the bottom, but before the spirit of wine is abstracted, the oil is blood red and a true quintessence.

AN EXCELLENT ESSENCE OF ANY VEGETABLE MAY BE MADE THUS

Take of the distilled oil of any vegetable and imbibe with it the best manna, being very well depurated, until it will imbibe no more. Then digest them a month, and you shall have the true balsam and excellent essence of any vegetable.

This has the virtues of the vegetable whereof it was made but in a more eminent manner.

The depuration of manna for this use is a great secret. .

WATER OR SPIRIT OF MANNA IS MADE THUS

Take of the best manna one part, of nitre two parts. Put them into an ox bladder and, tying it close, put it into warm water to be dissolved. Distill this water in an alembic, and there will come forth an insipid water, sudorific and laxative.

THE CHEMICAL OIL OF THE HERB OR FLOWER OF ANY VEGETABLE IS MADE THUS

Take of the herb or flower dried one pound, of spring water twenty four pints, and distill them in a great alembic with its cooler or copper still with a worm passing through a vessel of cold water. Let the oil that is drawn with the water be separated with a tunnel or separating glass, and let the water that is separated be kept for a new distillation.
Note that if this water be used two or three times in the drawing of the oil, it will be an excellent water of that vegetable from which it is distilled, and as good as most that shall be drawn any other way.
After the same manner are made oil of the dry rinds of oranges, citrons, and lemons.

But note that these rinds must be fresh and (the inward whiteness being separated) be bruised.

THE OIL COMMONLY CALLED THE SPIRIT OF ROSES

Take of damask or red roses, being fresh, as many as you please. Infuse them in as much warm water as is sufficient for the space of 24 hours. Then strain and press them and repeat the infusion several times with pressing until the liquor becomes fully impregnated, which then must be distilled in an alembic with a refrigeratory or copper still with a worm. Let the spirit which swims on the water be separated, and the water kept for a new infusion.

This kind of spirit may be made by bruising the roses with salt, or laying a lane of roses and another of salt, and so keeping them half a year or more, which then must be distilled in as much common water or rose water as is sufficient.

OILS ARE MADE OUT OF SEEDS THUS

Take of what seeds you please, bruised, two pounds. Of spring water take twenty pints, let them be macerated for the space of 24 hours, and then be distilled in a copper still with a worm or alembic with its refrigerating. The oil extracted with the water, being separated with a tunnel, keep the water for a new distillation.

This water after three or four distillations is a very excellent water and better than is drawn any way out of that vegetable whereof these are seeds; I mean for virtue though not always for smell.

After the same manner are made oils of spices and aromatical woods.

OILS ARE MADE OUT OF BERRIES THUS

Take of what berries you please, being fresh, 25 pounds. Bruise them and put them into a wooden vessel with 12 pinte of spring water and and a pound of the strongest leaven. Let them be put in a cellar (the vessel being close stopped) for the space of three months. Then let them be distilled in an alembic or copper still with their refrigeratory with as much spring water as is sufficient. After the separation of the oil, let the water be kept for a new distillation. Note that the water

being used in two or three distillations is a very excellent water and full
of the virtue of the berries.

OIL IS MADE OUT OF ANY SOLID WOOD THUS

Take of what wood you please, made into gross powder, as much as
you will. Let it be put into a retort and distilled in sand. The oil which
first distills, as being the thinner and sweeter, must be kept apart which,
with rectifying with much water, may yet be made more pleasant. The
acid water or spirit which in distilling comes first forth, being separated,
which also (being rectified from the phlegm with the heat of a
balneum) may be kept for use, being full of the virtue of the wood.
After the same manner are made the oil and spirit of tartar, but thus
much note, that both are more pure and pleasant being made out of the
crystals than out of the crude tartar.

TO MAKE A MOST EXCELLENT OIL OUT OF ANY WOOD
OR GUMS IN A SHORT TIME WITHOUT MUCH COST

Take of what wood you please or gum bruised small. Put it into a vessel
fit for it. Then pour on so much of spirit of salt as will cover your
matter. Then set it in sand with an alembic. Make the spirit boil so all
the oil flies over with a little phlegm, for the spirit of salt by its
sharpness frees the oil so that it flies over very easily.
The spirit of salt being rectified may serve again.

TO MAKE VEGETABLES YIELD THEIR OIL EASILY

Distill them, being first bruised, in salt water, for salt frees the oil from
its body. Let them first be macerated three or four days in the said
water.

OIL OR SPIRIT OF TURPENTINE IS MADE THUS

Take of Venice turpentine as much as you please, and of spring water
four times as much. Let them be put into an alembic or copper still
with its refrigeratory. Then put fire under it. So there will distill a thin
white oil like water, and in the bottom of the vessel will remain a hard
gum called Colophonia, which is called boiled turpentine. That white

oil may be better and freer from the smell of the fire if it be drawn in balneum with a gourd and glass-head.

Common oil of olive may be distilled after this manner and be made very pleasant and sweet, also most unctious things, as spermaceti, storax liquid, and also many gums.

OIL OF GUMS, RESINS, FAT AND OILY THINGS MAY BE DRAWN THUS

Take of either of these which you please, being melted, a pound, and and mix it with three pounds of the powder of tiles or unslaked lime. Put them into a retort and extract an oil which with plenty of water may be rectified.

Note that the water from whence the oil is separated is of excellent virtue, according to the nature of the matter from whence it is drawn.

OIL OF CAMPHOR IS MADE THUS

Take of camphor sliced thin as much as you please and put it into a double quantity of aqua fortis or spirit of wine. Let the glass, having a narrow neck, be set by the fire or on sand or ashes the space of five or six hours, shaking the glass every half hour, and the camphor will all be dissolved and swim on the aqua fortis or spirit of wine like an oil. Note that if you separate it, it will all be hard again presently, but not otherwise.

ANOTHER WAY TO MAKE OIL OF CAMPHOR THAT IT SHALL NOT BE REDUCED AGAIN

Take of camphor powdered as much as you please and put it into a glass like a urinal. Put upon it another urinal-glass inverted, the joints being close shut. Sublime it in ashes, inverting those urinals so often until the camphor be turned into an oil. Then circulate it for the space of a month, and it will be so subtle that it will all presently vapor away in the air, if the glass be open.

ANOTHER WAY TO MAKE OIL OF CAMPHOR

Take two ounces of camphor and dissolve it in four ounces of pure oil of olive. Then put them into four pints of fair water and distill them all together in a glass gourd, either in ashes or balneum, and there will distill both water and oil, which separate and keep by itself.

All these kinds of oil of camphor are very good against putrefaction, fits of the mother, passions of the heart, etc. A few drops thereof may be taken in any liquor, or the breast be annointed therewith. Also, the fume thereof may be taken in at the mouth

A TRUE OIL OF SUGAR

Take of the best white sugar candy and imbibe it with the best spirit of wine ten times, after every time drying it again. Then hang it in a white silken bag in a moist cellar over a glass vessel that it may dissolve and drop into it. Evaporate the water in balneum, and in the bottom will the oil remain.

This is very excellent in all distempers of the lungs.

OIL OF AMBER IS MADE THUS

Take of yellow amber one part, of the powder of flints calcined, or the powder of tiles two parts. Mingle them, put them into a retort, and distill them in sand. The oil which is white and clear that first distilled off, keep by itself, continuing the distillation as long as any oil distills off. Then let both oils be rectified apart in a good quantity of water. The salt of amber, which adheres to the neck of the retort withinside, being gathered, let be purified by solution, filtration, and coagulation according to art, and kept for use.

After this manner may be made oils out of any gums which may be powdered.

OIL OF MYRRH IS MADE THUS

Take of myrrh bruised or bay-salt, of each six pounds. Let them be dissolved in sixty pints of spring water and be distilled in an alembic or copper still according to art.

OIL OF MYRRH PER DELIQUIUM OR BY DISSOLUTION IS MADE THUS

Take hen eggs hard boiled and cut in the middle lengthways. Take out the yolks, then fill up the hollow half way with powder of myrrh, and join the parts together again, binding them with a thread. Set them upon a grate between two platters in a cold moist place, so the liquor of the myrrh dissolved will distill into the lower platter.

OIL OF TARTAR PER DELIQUIUM, BY DISSOLUTION

Take of the best tartar calcined white according to art. Put it into a cotton bag, and hang it in the cellar or some moist place, putting under it a receiver.

OILS OF EXPRESSION ARE MADE THUS

Take of what things you please, such as will afford an oil by expression. Bruise them, then put them into a bag, and press them strongly, putting a vessel under to receive the oil.
Note that they must stand in the press some hours, because the oil drops by little and little.

Note also that if you warm them before you put them into the press, they will yield more oil, but then it will not keep so long as otherwise. After this manner are made oils of nutmegs, mace, almonds, linseed, and such like.

A VOMITING & PURGING OIL MADE BY EXPRESSION

Take of the berries of ebulus or dwarf elder, as many as you please. Let them be dried but not over much. Then bruise them, and in bruising them, moisten them with the best spirit of wine until they begin to be oily. Then warm them by the fire, and press forth the oil, and set it in the sun putrefied.

Ten drops of this oil taken inwardly works upward and downward, and is very good against the dropsy and all waterish diseases.
The belly being therewith anointed is made thereby soluble.
Any part that is much pained with the gout or any such grief is presently eased by being anointed with this oil.

OIL OF JASMINE IS MADE THUS

Take of flowers of jasmine as many as you please, and put them into as much sweet mature oil as you please. Put them into a glass close stopped, and set them into the sun to be infused for the space of 20 days. Then take them out and strain the oil from the flowers and, if you would have the oil yet stronger, put in new flowers and do as before. This is a pleasant perfume and being mixed with oils and ointments gives them a grateful smell. It is also used in the perfuming of leather. After this manner may be made oil of any flowers. But because I shall keep myself to the art of distillation only, I shall not so far digress as to speak of these kinds of oils, only I thought it good to set down the oil of jasmine because by reason of its fragrancy it has some analogy with chemical oils that are made by distillation.

TO MAKE ANY OIL OR WATER PER DESCENSUM

Take an earthen gourd and fill it full with wood or herbs, or what you please, being cut small. Then invert it, set it in a furnace, and lute it well "hereunto. Then set another gourd of earth under it with a wider mouth that the uppermost may go into it. Before you put the one into the other, you must have a little vessel or instrument of tin with brims around about on the top, by which it must hang into the lower gourd, the body thereof being two or three inches deep and full of holes, so that the oil or water may drop through and not the vegetable itself. Into this instrument, being first set into the lower gourd, put the mouth of the upper gourd. Then make your fire on the top and keep it burning as long as any liquor will drop.

The figure of the furnace is thus.

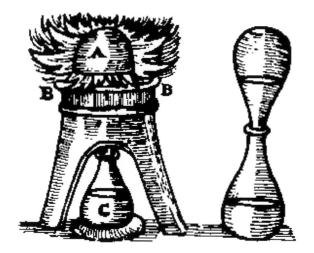

A. Signifies the gourd containing the matter to be distilled.
B. The furnace containing the coals, so that they surround the upper gourd.
C. The lower gourd or recipient set upon straw rings.
D. The vessel of tin with holes and brims which must be set in the recipient.

HOW TO MAKE AN OIL AND WATER OUT OF SOOT

This may be distilled per descensum or by retort as thus, viz., take of the best soot (which shines like jet) and fill with it a glass retort coated or earthen retort to the neck. Distill it with a strong fire by degrees into a large receiver, and there will come forth a yellowish spirit with a black oil which you may separate and digest.

HOW TO RECTIFY SPIRITS

You must set them in the sun in glasses well stopped, and half filled, being set in sand to the third part of their height that the water waxing hot by the heat of the sun may separate itself from the phlegm mixed therewith which will be performed in 12 or 15 days. There is another better way to do this which is to distill them again in balneum with a gentle fire, or if you will put them into a retort furnished with its receiver and set them upon crystal or iron bowls, or in an iron mortar directly opposite the beams of the sun, as you may learn by these ensuing signs.

A retort with its receiver standing upon crystal bowls just opposite to the sun beams.

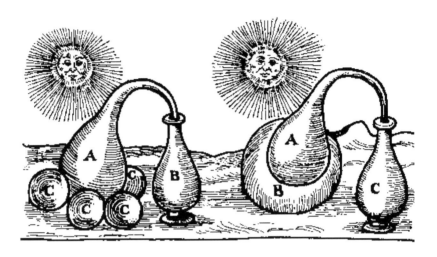

A. Shows the retort.
B. Shows the receiver.
C. The crystal bowls.

Another retort with its receiver standing in a marble or iron mortar directly opposite the sun.

A. Shows the retort.
B. The marble or iron mortar
C. The receiver.

HOW TO RECTIFY ALL STINKING THICK BLACK OILS THAT ARE MADE BY A RETORT AND TO TAKE AWAY THEIR STINK

Take oil of amber, or any such stinking oil, put it into a glass retort, the fourth part only being full, pour on it drop by drop the spirit of salt (or any other acid spirit) and they will boil together. When so much of the spirit is poured on that it boils no more, then cease and distill it. First comes over a stinking water, then a clear white, well smelling oil, and after that a yellow oil which is indifferent good. But the spirit of salt has lost its sharpness. The volatile salt of the oil remains coagulated with the spirit of salt and is black and tastes like sal ammoniac, and has no smell being sublimed from it. Now the reason of all this is, because the volatile salt of the oil, which is the cause of the stink thereof, is fixed by the acid spirit of the salt; for acid spirits and volatile salts are contrary the one to the other, and spirit of urine or any volatile salt will precipitate any metal as well as salt of tartar.

These oils will remain clear and have far more virtue than the ordinary sort of oils have.

As for common ordinary distilled oils, they need not, if they be well separated from the water with which they were distilled, any rectifying at all. If you go about to rectify them, you will lose a good part of them and make that which remains not at all the better. But if there be any better than another for rectifying of them it is by digestion, by which you may separate afterwards, and by this means you shall lose none of the oils.

BOOK II

OF COMPOUND WATERS AND SPIRITS

A DISSOLVING MENSTRUUM

Take cyprus, turpentine, and the best spirit of wine, of each two pounds. Distill them in a glass gourd either in balneum or ashes. Separate the oil from the spirit with a tunnel or separating glass. Distill the spirit again and so often until it favors no more of the oil of turpentine, and then it is sufficiently prepared.

This menstruum dissolves any hard stones presently, and extracts the tincture of coral.

A glass gourd with its head.

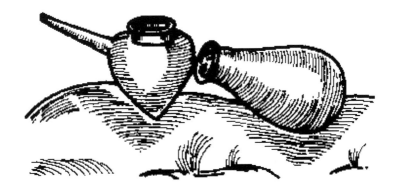

ANOTHER DISSOLVING MENSTRUUM OR ACETUM PHILOSOPHICUM

Take honey, salt melted, of each one pound, and of the strongest spirit of vinegar two pounds. Digest them for the space of a fortnight or more. Then distill them in ashes, cohobate the liquor upon the feces

three or four times, and then rectify the spirit.
Note that they must be done in a large glass gourd.

This is of the same virtue as the former, if not more powerful.

ANOTHER DISSOLVING MENSTRUUM

Take of the best rectified spirit of wine with which imbibe the strongest
unslaked lime until they be made into a paste. Then put them into a
glass gourd and distill off the spirit in ashes. This spirit pour on more
fresh lime, and do as before. Do this three or four times and you will
have a very subtle spirit able to dissolve most things and to extract the
virtue out of them.

PARACELSUS HIS ELIXIR SUBTILITATIS

Take oil of olive, honey, rectified spirit of wine, of each a pint. Distill
them all together in ashes. Then separate all the phlegm from the oils
which will be distinguished by many colors. Put all these colors into a
pelican, and add to them the third part of the essence of balm and
sallendine, and digest them for the space of a month. Then keep it for
use. The liquor is so subtle that it penetrates everything.

USQUE - BATH OR IRISH AQUA VITAE IS MADE THUS

Take a gallon of small aqua vitae and put it into a glass vessel. Put
thereto a quart of canary sack, two pounds of raisins of the sun stoned,
but not washed, two ounces of dates stoned, and the white skins thereof
pulled out, two ounces of cinnamon grossly bruised, four good nutmegs
bruised, an ounce of the best english licorice sliced and bruised. Stop
the vessels very close and let them infuse in a cold place six or eight
days. Then let the liquor run through a bag called Manica Hippocratis
made of white cotton.

This liquor is commonly used in surfeits, being a good stomach water.

AQUA CELESTIS IS MADE THUS

Take of cinnamon, cloves, ginger, nutmegs, zedoary, galangal, long pepper, citron pill, spikenard, lignum aloes, cububs, cardamum, calamus aromaticus, germander, ground pine, mace, white frankincense, tormentil, hermodactyls, the pith of dwarf elder, juniper berries, bay berries, the seeds and flowers of motherwort, the seeds of smallage, the seeds of fennel, seeds of anise, the leaves of sorrel, the leaves of sage, the leaves of felwort, rosemary, marJoram, mints, pennyroyal, stechados, the flowers of elder, the flowers of red roses, the flowers of white roses, of the leaves of scabious, rue, the lesser moonwort, agrimony, centory, fumitory, pimpernel, sow thistle, eyebright, maidenhair, endive, red launders, aloes - of each two ounces, pure amber, the best rhubarb - of each two drams, dried figs, raisins of the sun, stoned dates, sweet almonds, grains of the pine - of each an ounce.

Of the best aqua vitae to the quantity of them all, of the best hard sugar a pound, of white honey half a pound. Then add the root of gentian, flowers of rosemary, pepperwort, the root of briony, sow bread, wormwood - of each half an ounce.

Now before these are distilled, quench gold being made red hot, oftentimes in the aforesaid water, put therein oriental pearls beaten small an ounce, and then distill it after 24 hours infusion.

This is a very cordial water, good against faintings and infection.

AQUA IMPERIALIS IS MADE THUS

Take of the rind of citrons dried, oranges, nutmeg, cloves, cinnamon - of each two ounces; of each half a pound of the roots of flowers-de-luce, the roots of cyprus, the roots of calamus aromaticus, the roots of zedoary, the roots of galangal, the roots of ginger; two handsful each of the tops of lavender, the tops of rosemary; of the leaves of the bay tree, of the leaves of marjoram, of the leaves of balm, of the leaves of mint, of the leaves of sage, of the leaves of thyme, flowers of white roses, flowers of damask roses, of each half a handful; rose water, four pints; the best white wine, a gallon.

Bruise what must be bruised. Then infuse them all 24 hours, after which distill them.

This is of the same virtue as the former.

AQUA MIRABILIS IS MADE THUS

Take a dram each of cloves, galangal, cububs, mace, cardamum, nutmeg, and ginger; half a pint of the juice of sallendine; a pint of the spirit of wine; three pints of white wine. Infuse all these 24 hours, and then distill off two pints by alembic. This water is very good against wind in the stomach and head.

DR. STEPHEN'S WATER IS MADE THUS

Take a gallon of gascoigne wine; a dram each of ginger, galganal, cinnamon, nutmeg, grains, aniseed, fennel seeds, carroway seeds; a handful each of sage, red mints, red roses, thyme, pellitory, rosemary, wild thyme, chamomile, and lavender.
Beat the spices small and bruise the herbs, letting them macerate 12 hours, stirring them now and then. Distill them by an alembic or copper still with its refrigeratory. Keep the first pint by itself, and the second by itself.
Note that the first pint will be hotter, but the second the stronger of the ingredients.
This water is well known to comfort all the principal parts.

A FAMOUS SURFEIT WATER

Take of red poppy cakes (after the water has been distilled from them in a cold still) not over dried two pounds. Pour upon them of the water of red poppy a gallon and a half, canary wine three pints. Add to them of coriander seeds bruised four ounces, of dill seed bruised two ounces, of cloves bruised half an ounce, of nutmeg sliced an ounce, of rosemary a handful, three oranges cut in the middle. Distill them in a hot still. To the water put the juice of six oranges and hang in it half an ounce of nutmeg sliced and as much cinnamon bruised, two drams of cloves, a handful of rosemary cut small, sweet fennel seeds bruised an ounce, of raisins of the sun stoned half a pound, being all put into a bag, which may be hung in the water (the vessel being close stopped) the space of a month, and then be taken out and cast away, the liquor thereof being first pressed out into the foresaid water.

This water is of wonderful virtue in surfeits and pleurisies, composes the spirits, causes rest, helps digestion if two or three or four ounces thereof be drunk, and the patient composes himself to rest.

A PECTORAL WATER

Distill green hysop in a cold still until you have a gallon and a half of the water. To this put four handfuls of dried hysop, a handful of rue, as much of rosemary, and horehound, elecampane root, bruised, and of horse-radish root, bruised, of each four ounces, of tobacco in the leaf three ounces, aniseed bruised two ounces, two quarts of canary wine. Let them all stand in digestion two days and then distill them. In the water that is distilled put half a pound of raisins of the sun stoned, of licorice two ounces, sweet fennel seeds bruised two ounces and a half, ginger sliced an ounce and a half. Let them be infused in frigido the space of ten days. Then take them out.

This water sweetened with sugar candy and drunk to the quantity of three or four ounces twice in a day is very good for those that are ptisical. It strengthens the lungs, attenuates thick phlegm, opens obstructions, and is very good to comfort the stomach.

A VERY EXCELLENT WATER AGAINST THE WORMS

Take of worm seed eight ounces, the shavings of harts-horn two ounces, of peach flowers dried an ounce, of aloes bruised half an ounce. Pour on these the water of tansy, rue, peach flowers, and of wormwood, of each a pint and a half. Let them, being put into a glass vessel be digested the space of three days. Then distill them. Cohobate this water three times. This water is very excellent against the worms. It may be given from half an ounce to 3 ounces, according to the age of the patient.

A WATER AGAINST THE CONVULSIONS

Take of ros vitriol (which is that water that is distilled from vitriol in the calcining thereof) two quarts. In this put of rue a handful, juniper berries bruised an ounce, of bay berries bruised half an ounce, piony berries bruised six drams, camphor two drams, rhubarb sliced an ounce. Digest these four days in a temperate balneum. Then distill them in a glass vessel in ashes, and there will come over a water of no small virtue. It cures convulsions in children, especially. It helps also the vertigo, the hysterical passion, and epilepsy. It is very excellent against all offensive vapors and wind that annoys the head and stomach.
It may be taken from two drams to two ounces.

A HYDROPICAL WATER

Take of wormwood, broom blossoms, of each a like quantity. Bruise them and mix with them some leaven and let them stand in fermentation in a cold place the space of a week. Then distill them in a cold still until they be very dry. Take a gallon of this water and half a gallon of the spirit of urine. Pour them upon two pounds of dried broom blossoms, half a pound of horse-radish roots dried, three ounces of the best rhubarb sliced, two ounces of sweet fennel seed bruised, and an ounce and a half of nutmeg. Let them digest a week, being put into a glass vessel in a temperate balneum. Then press the liquor hard from the feces. Put this liquor in the said vessel again and to it put three ounces of sweet fennel seeds bruised, licorice sliced two ounces. Digest them in a gentle heat for the space of a week. Then pour it off from the feces and keep it close stopped.

This water being drunk from the quantity of an ounce to four ounces every morning, and at four of the clock in the afternoon, does seldom fail in curing the dropsie. It strengthens also the liver, is very good against gravel in the back, stone, cures the scurvy, gout, and such diseases as proceed from the weakness and obstructions of the liver.

A WATER AGAINST THE COLIC

Take of aniseed 3 ounces, cumin seed 3 drams, cinnamon half an ounce, mace, cloves, nutmeg, of each a dram, galangal, 3 drams, calamus aromaticus, dried, half an ounce, the dried rind of oranges, 2 ounces, bayberries, half an ounce.

Let all these, being bruised, be macerated in six pints of mallago wine, and then be distilled in balneum until all be dry.
This water being drunk to the quantity of an ounce or two at a time does ease the gripings of the belly and stomach very much.

A WATER AGAINST THE VERTIGO AND CONVULSIONS

Take of black cherries bruised with their kernels, a gallon; of the flowers of lavender, 3 handfuls; half an ounce of white mustard seed bruised. Mix these together and then put some ferment to them and let them stand close covered the space of a week. Then distill them in balneum until all be dry.

The water being drunk to the quantity of an ounce or two or three does much relieve the weakness of the head and helps the vertigo thereof, as also strengthens the sinews, and expels windiness out of the head and stomach.

A COMPOUND WATER OF BURRE ROOT CAUSING SWEAT

Take the root of the great burre fresh, the root of the swallow wort fresh, and the middle rind of the root of the ash tree; of each two pounds.

Cut them small and infuse them 24 hours in the best white wine and rue vinegar, of each five pints. Then distill them in balneum until all be dry. Put to the water as much of the spirit of sulphur per campanam as will give it a pleasant acidity, and to every pint of the water put a scruple and a half of camphor cut small and tied up in a bag which may continually hang in the water.

This was a famous water in Germany against the plague, pestilential and epidemical diseases. It causes sweat wonderful if two or three ounces thereof be drunk and the patient composes himself to sweat.

ANOTHER EXCELLENT SUDORIFIC AND PLAGUE WATER

Take of the best spirit of wine, a gallon; andromachus-treakle, six
ounces; myrrh, two ounces; the roots of colts foot, three ounces;
spermaceti, terra sigillata, of each half an ounce; the root of swallow
wort, an ounce; dittany, pimpernell, valerian root, of each two drams;
camphor a dram.

Mix all these together in a glass vessel, and let them stand close stopped
the space of 8 days in the sun.

Let the patient drink of this a spoonful or two and compose himself to
sweat.

DR. BURGES, HIS PLAGUE WATER

Take three pints of muscadine and boil in it sage and rue, of each a
handful, until a pint be wasted. Then strain it and set it over the fire
again. Put thereto a dram of long pepper, ginger, and nutmeg, of each
half an ounce, being all bruised together. Then boil them a little and
put thereto half an ounce of andromachus-treakle, and three drams of
mithridate, and a quarter of a pint of the best angelica water.
This water (which, as says the author, must be kept as your life, and
above all earthly treasure) must be taken to the quantity of a spoonful
or two morning and evening, if you be already infected, and sweat
thereupon. If you be not infected, a spoonful is sufficient, half in the
morning and half at night. All the plague time under God (says the
author) trust to this, for there was never man, woman, or child that
failed of their expectation in taking it. This is also of the same efficacy,
not only against the plague, but pox, measles, surfeits, etc.

CROLLIUS, HIS TREAKLE WATER CAMPHORATED

Take of andromachus, his treakle, five ounces; the best myrrh, two
ounces and a half; the best saffron, half an ounce; camphor, two drams.
Mix them together. Then pour upon them ten ounces of the best spirit
of wine, and let them stand 24 hours in a warm place. Then distill them
in balneum with a gradual fire. Cohobate the spirit three times.

This spirit causes sweat wonderfully and resists all manner of infection. It may be taken from a dram to an ounce in some appropriate liquor.

A DISTILLED TREAKLE VINEGAR

Take of the roots of bistort, gentian, angelica, tormentil, pimpernel, of each 10 drams; bay berries, juniper berries, of each an ounce; nutmeg, five drams; the shavings of sassafras, two ounces; zedoary, half a dram; white sanders, three drams; the leaves of rue, wormwood, scordium, of each half a handful; the flowers of wall flower, bugloss, of each a handful and a half; andromachus treakle, mithridate, of each six drams. Infuse them all in three pints of the best white wine vinegar for the space of 8 days in frigido in glass vessels. Then distill them in balneum. The spirit is very good to prevent them that are free from infection, and those that are already infected, from the danger thereof, if two or three spoonfuls thereof be taken once a day, with sweating after, for those that are infected, but without sweating for others.

AN EXCELLENT WATER AGAINST THE STONE IN THE KIDNEYS

Take of the middle rind of the root of ash, bruised, 2 pounds; juniper berries, bruised, 3 pounds; venice turpentine that is very pure, 2 pounds and a half.

Put these into 12 pints of spring water in a glass vessel well closed, and there let them putrify in horse dung for the space of three months. Then distill them in ashes and there will come forth an oil and a water. Separate the one from the other.

Ten or twelve drops of this oil being taken every morning in four or six spoonfuls of the said water dissolves the gravel and stone in the kidneys most wonderfully.

ANOTHER WATER FOR THE SAME USE

Take the juice of radishes and lemons, of each a pound and a half; waters of betony, tansy, saxifrage, and vervain, of each a pint; hydromel and malmefey, of each two pounds. In these liquors mixed together, infuse for the space of 4 or 5 days in a gentle balneum, juniper berries, ripe and newly gathered, being bruised, 3 ounces; the seed of gromwell, burdock, radish, saxifrage, nettles, onions, anise, and fennel, of each an ounce and a half; the four cold seeds, the seed of great mallows, of each six drams; the calx of egg shells, cinnamon, of each three drams; of camphor two drams. Let all be well strained and distilled in ashes.

Two ounces of this water taken every morning does wonderfully cleanse the kidneys, provoke urine, and expel the stone, especially if you calcine the feces and extract the salt thereof with the said water.

TO MAKE AN EXCELLENT WOUND WATER

Take plantain, rib wort, bone wort, wild angelica, red mints, betony, agrimony, sanicle, blue bottles, white bottles, scabious, dandelion, evens, honeysuckle leaves, bramble buds, hawthorne buds and leaves, mugwort, daisy roots, leaves and flowers, wormwood, southern wood, of each one handful. Boil all these in a bottle of white wine and as much spring water, until one half be wasted. When it is thus boiled, strain it from the herbs and put to it half a pound of honey and let it boil a little after. Then put into bottles and keep it for your use.

Note that these herbs must be gathered in May only, but you may keep them dry and make your water at any time.

This water is very famous in many countries, and it has done such cures in curing outward and inward wounds, impostumes, and ulcers that you would scarce believe it if I should recite them to you. Also it is very good to heal a sore mouth.

The patient must take three or four spoonfuls thereof morning and evening, and in a short time he shall find ease and indeed a cure, unless he be so far declined as nothing almost can recover him.

If the wound be outward, it must be washed therewith, and the linen clothes wet in the same be applied thereto.

DR. MATHIAS, HIS PALSY WATER IS MADE THUS

Take of lavender flowers a gallon and pour upon them of the best spirit of wine, three gallons. The vessel being close stopped, let them be macerated together in the sun for the space of sex days. Then distill them in alembic with its refrigeratory. Then take the flowers of sage, rosemary, betony, of each a handful; borage, bugloss, lillies of the valley, cowslips, of each two handfuls.

Let the flowers be fresh, and seasonably gathered, and macerated in a gallon of the beat spirits of wine and mixed with the aforesaid spirit of lavender. Then add the leaves of balm, motherwort, orange tree newly gathered, the flowers of stechados, oranges, bayberries, of each an ounce.

After a convenient digestion let them be distilled again. Then add the outward rinds of citrons, the seed of peony husked, of each six drams; cinnamon, nutmeg, mace, cardamum, cububs, of yellow sanders, of each half an ounce; lignum aloes, one dram; the best jujube, the kernels taken out, half a pound.

Let them be digested for the space of six weeks. Then strain and filter the liquor to which add of prepared pearl two drams; prepared emerald, a scruple; ambergris, musk, saffron, red roses, launders, of each an ounce; yellow sanders, rinds of citrons dried, of each a dram.
Let all these species be tied in a silken bag and hung in the foresaid spirit.

A SCORBUTICAL WATEROR A COMPOUND WATER OF HORSERADISH IS MADE THUS

Take the leaves of both scurvy grass, being made very clean, of each six pounds. Let these be bruised and the juice pressed forth, to which add the juice of brook lime, watercress, of each half a pound; of the best white wine, eight pints; twelve whole lemons cut; of the fresh roots of briony, four pounds; horseradish, two pounds; of nutmeg, four ounces. Let them be macerated three days and distilled.

Three or four spoonfuls of this water taken twice in a day cures the scurvy presently.

SPIRIT OF CASTOR IS MADE THUS

Take of fresh castoreum, two ounces; flowers of lavender, fresh, half an ounce; sage, rosemary, of each two drams; cinnamon, three drams; mace, cloves, of each a dram; the best rectified spirit of wine, three pints. Let them be digested in a glass (two parts of three being empty) stopped close with a bladder, and cork two days in warm ashes. Then distill the spirit in balneum, and keep it in a glass close stopped. If you would make it stronger, take a pint of this spirit and an ounce of the powder of castoreum. Put them into a glass and digest them into a cold place for space of ten days, and then strain out the spirit.

This spirit is very good against fits of the mother, passions of the heart which arise from vapors, etc.

BEZEARD WATER IS MADE THUS

Take of the leaves of the greater sallandine together with the roots thereof, three handfuls and a half; of rue, two handfuls; scordium, four handfuls; dittany of Crete, Carduus, of each a handful and a half; root of zedoary, angelica, of each three drams; the outward rind of citrons, lemons, of each six drams; the flower of wall gilly flower, an ounce and a half; red roses, the lesser centory, of each two drams; cinnamon, cloves, of each three drams; andromachus, his treakle, three ounces; mithridate, an ounce and a half; camphor, two scruples; trochisces of vipers, two ounces; mace, two drams; lignum aloes, half an ounce; yellow sanders, a dram and a half; the seeds of carduus, an ounce; citron, six drams.

Cut those things that are to be cut, and let them be macerated three days in the best spirit of wine and muscadine, of each three pints and a half; vinegar of wall gilly flowers and the juice of lemons, of each a pint. Let them be distilled in a glazed vessel in balneum.

After half the liquor is distilled off, let that which remains in the vessel be strained through a linen cloth and vapored away to the thickness of honey which may be called a Bezeard extract.

This water is a great cordial and good against any infection.

TO MAKE A SPECIFIC SUDORIFIC

Take of ginger a pound; long pepper and black pepper, of each half an ounce; of cardamums, three drams; of grains, an ounce. Powder them and put them into a glass with half an ounce of the best camphor; distilled vinegar, two pounds; digest them a month and then separate the vinegar by expression which must putrefy a month and then be circulated for the space of a week. Then filter it and you have as powerful a sudorific as ever was or can be made.
The dose is from a dram to half an ounce, and to be drunk in a draught of posset drink.

TREAKLE WATER IS MADE THUS

Take the juice of the green shells of walnuts four pounds, the juice of rue three pints, carduus, marigold, balm, of each two pints. The root of butter burr fresh, a pound and a half, burr, angelica, master wort fresh, of each half a pound. The leaves of scordium, four handfuls. Old andromachus treakle, mithridate, of each eight ounces, the best canarie, twelve pints, the sharpest vinegar, six pints. the juice of lemons, two pints.

Digest them two days in horse dung, the vessel being close stopped. Then distill them in sand.

AQUA MARIAE IS MADE THUS

Take of sugar candid, one pound; canarie wine, six ounces; rose water, four ounces. Make of these a syrup and boil it well, to which add of aqua imperialis, two pints; ambergris, musk, of each eighteen grains; yellow sanders, infused in aqua imperialis, two drams.

THE MOTHER WATER COMMONLY CALLED HYSTERICAL WATER IS MADE THUS

Take of the juice of the root of briony four pounds.
Leaves of rue, mugwort, of each two pounds. savin dried, three handfuls. motherwort, nippe, pennyroyal, of each two handfuls. garden basil, dittany of Crete, of each a handful and a half. The rind of yellow

oranges, fresh, four ounces. myrrh, two ounces. castoreum, an ounce. best canarie wine, twelve pints.

Let them be distilled four days in a fit vessel. Then distill them in balneum.

A VOMITING WATER IS MADE THUS

Take of the best tobacco in leaves, cut small, four ounces; squils, two ounces; nutmeg sliced, half an ounce. Put these into three pints of spring water, a pint of white wine vinegar. Distill them in a hot still or alembic.

If you would have it stronger, you must put this water on fresh ingredients and distill it again.

A little quantity of this water is a most safe and effectual vomit, and may be taken from the eldest to the youngest, if so be you proportion the quantity to the strength of the patient.

You may dulcify it with sugar or syrup if you please.

A VOMITING WATER MADE BY PLATEAUS

Take of green walnuts gathered about midsummer, radish root, of each bruised, two parts; of distilled wine vinegar, four parts. Digest them five days, then distill them in balneum.

This being taken to the quantity of two spoonfuls, or three, causes easy vomiting.

A DISTILLED WATER THAT PURGES WITHOUT ANY PAIN OR GRIPING

Take of scammony an ounce; hermodactyles, two ounces; the seeds of broom, of the lesser spurge, of dwarf elder, of each half an ounce; the juice of dwarf elder, of wild asses cucumber, of black hellebore, the fresh flower of elder, of each an ounce and a half; polypodium, six ounces; of sene, three ounces; red sugar, eight ounces; common distilled

water, six pints.
Let all these be bruised and infused in the water 24 hours, then be
distilled in balneum.

This water may be given from two drams to three ounces, and it purges
all manner of humors, opens all obstructions, and is pleasant to be
taken. Those whose stomachs loathe all other physics may take this
without any offence.

After it is distilled there may be a little bag of spices in it, as also it may
be sweetened with sugar or any opening syrup.

A SPECIFIC LIQUOR AGAINST THE TOOTHACHE

Take of oil of cloves well rectified half an ounce. In it dissolve half a
dram of camphor. Add to them of the spirit of turpentine, four times
rectified in which half a dram of opium has been infused, half an ounce.
A drop or two of this liquor put into a hollow tooth with some lint
eases the toothache presently.

BOOK III

OF MINERALS

SPIRIT OF SALT IS MADE THUS

Take of the best bay salt as much as you please. Let it be dissolved in spring water and filtered. Mix this with brine in a copper vessel, of the powder of bricks or tiles, twice or thrice as much as the salt before its dissolution was in weight; let the water vapor away over the fire (continually stirring of it) until it be dry. Then put this powder into a glass retort well luted, or an earthen retort, and put it into a furnace (a large receiver joined to it according to art). Then give fire to it by degrees until it will bear an open fire, for the space of 12 hours. You shall have a very acid oil or spirit in the receiver. That liquor, being put into a little retort in sand, may be rectified by the vaporing away of the phlegm. Then keep it for use in a glass very well stopped that no air goes in.

Spirit of salt is very good in fevers putrid, as in hydropical diseases.

A retort and its receiver before they be set on work.

A retort with its receiver set on work.

OIL OR SPIRIT OF SALT MAY ALSO BE MADE AFTER THIS MANNER

Take one part of salt and three parts of powder of bricks or tiles, mix them together, and put them into a retort either of glass or earth, to which put fire as before.

After this manner you may make oil or spirit of nitre, salt gem, alum. Note that these salts must first be calcined which is done by exhaling their phlegm.

TO TURN SALTPETRE INTO A WATER BY A MERE DIGESTION

Take of saltpetre powdered very small and with it fill the fourth part of a bolt head. Close it well and let it stand in the heat of ashes or sand the space of six weeks, and you shall see a good part of it turned into water. Continue it in the said heat until it be all dissolved.

This is of incomparable use in fevers and against worms or any putrefaction in the body, and is indeed a most rare secret.

SPIRIT OF SALT ARMONIAC

Dissolve sal ammoniac in distilled spirit of urine over a moderate heat. In this spirit let bricks beaten into small pieces and made red hot be quenched until they have imbibed all the water. Then make distillation in a retort in sand or in a naked fire.

This spirit is of greater strength than that of other salts.

OIL OR SPIRIT OF VITRIOL IS MADE THUS

Take of hungarian, or the best english vitriol, as much as you please. Let it be melted in an earthen vessel glazed, with a soft fire, that all the moisture may exhale, continually stirring of it, until it be brought into a yellow powder which must be put into a glass retort well luted or an earthen retort that will endure the fire. Fit a large receiver to the retort and close the joints well together. Then give it fire by degrees until the second day. Then make the strongest heat you can until the receiver which before was dark with fumes be clear again. Let the liquor that is distilled off be put into a little retort, and the phlegm be drawn off in sand. So will the oil be rectified which is most strong and ponderous, and must be kept by itself.

Many call that phlegm which is drawn off in rectifying, the spirit of vitriol.

This oil or spirit is very excellent in putrid fevers, resisting putrefaction. Also, it opens all obstructions and is very diuretical.

A RED AND HEAVY OIL OF VITRIOL

Take of calcined vitriol one part, flints grossly powdered, two parts. Of these with spirit of wine make a paste. Distill it in a retort and there will come forth a red heavy oil.

This is to be used rather about metals than in the body. Only if the scurfe on the head be anointed therewith two or three times in a week, it will fall off and the head be cured.

TO DULCIFY THE SPIRIT OF VITRIOL AND OF SALT

Take the spirit of vitriol, or of salt, and the best spirit of wine, of each half a pound. Distill them in a retort together three or four-times, and they will be united inseparably and become sweet.

Some put eight eight ounces of the best sugar candy to these spirits before they be thus distilled.

Ten or twenty drops of this compound spirit being taken in any appropriate liquor is very good in any putrid or epidemical disease.

GILLA THEOPHRASTI OR A MOST DELICATE VOMITING LIQUOR MADE OF VITRIOL

Take of crystals made out of copper or iron. Dissolve them in the acid phlegm that first comes forth in the distilling of common vitriol. Circulate them eight days.

This liquor must be taken in wine. It causes vomiting instantly, and is most excellent to cleanse and strengthen the stomach and to cure all such distempers that arise from thence, as salt defluxions, fevers, worms, headache, vertigo, the hysterical passion, and such like.

The dose is from a scruple to two scruples.

OIL OF SULPHUR PER CAMPANUM

Take a large iron vessel like a platter. Over it hang a glass bell that has a nose like the head of a cold still. Fill the lower vessel, being narrower than the compass of the bell or head, with brimstone or sulphur. Inflame it, so will the fume which arises from thence be condensed in the bell into a liquor which will drop down through the nose into the receiver.

Note that the bell must hang at such a distance from the other vessel that the flame of the sulphur touches it not, according to this following example.

If instead of this broad vessel, you take a large crucible and melt in it saltpetre and cast sulphur upon it thus melted, you shall make a great deal quicker dispatch.

This spirit is of the same nature, and has the same operations, as oil of vitriol.

THE OIL OF SULPHUR IS MADE AFTER A MORE PHILOSOPHICAL MANNER THUS

Take of crude sulphur as much as you please. Put it into a melting vessel to be dissolved over the fire. Being dissolved, pour it forth into seething hot water (this do ten or more times, remembering that the water must be always seething hot) and you shall see that the sulphur will be like butter. Then put it into a retort, pouring on it the best spirit of wine. Distill it with a soft fire, and there will come forth an oil of a golden color, of a good taste and smell which is the true balsam of sulphur. The oil that swims on the spirit must be separated.

This oil for the cure of all distempers of the lungs, for all fevers whether putrid or pentilential, and the cure of wounds and ulcers, is scarce to be equalled.

THE ESSENCE OF SULPHUR

Take of sulphur vivum as much as you please. Dissolve it as well as you can in aqua fortis (made of vitriol and saltpetre). Then evaporate the aqua fortis, and then reverberate the matter until it becomes very red. Extract the tincture with spirit of wine, and then digest them until the essence be separated from the spirit like an oil and sink to the bottom. This essence also is of wonderful virtue against all putrefaction both inward and outward, a great preservative against the plague, and is wonderful balsamical, and cures all sores both old and new, even to admiration.

THE OIL OF ARSENIC IS MADE THUS

Take of crystalline arsenic (being first sublimed with colcothar alone) as much as you please. Mix it with an equal weight of the salt of tartar, and saltpetre. Let them be between two little pots or crucibles (whereof the upper has a hole) calcined until no fume ascends. The matter being thus calcined dissolve in warm water that you may draw a salt from thence. The powder which falls to the bottom imbibe with the liquor of tartar, and dry it by the fire. This you must do three times. Then dissolve the matter in warm water that you may draw out the salt thereof, and there will remain a most white powder, and fixed, which in a moist place will be dissolved into a liquid matter like oil or butter.

AQUA FORTIS OR A STRONG SPIRIT (THAT WILL DISSOLVE SILVER AND BASER METALS) IS MADE THUS

Take of vitriol calcined two parts and of nitre one part. Grind and mix them well together and put them into a glass retort coated or earthen retort that will endure the fire. Set them into the furnace in an open fire and then, having fitted a large receiver, distill it by degrees the space of 24 hours. Then rectify the water or spirit in sand.

AQUA REGIA OR STYGIA OR A STRONG SPIRIT THAT WILL DISSOLVE GOLD IS MADE THUS

Take of nitre two parts, salt armoniac one part, and the powder of flints three parts. Put them into a glass retort coated or earthen retort that will endure the fire. Distill them by degrees over a naked fire for the space of 24 hours. Take it out and rectify it. This water will dissolve gold.

ANOTHER AQUA REGIA IS MADE THUS

Take of spirit of nitre as much as you please. Put a dram of crude nitre to every ounce of it, and it will be as strong as any aqua regia. This water will dissolve gold.

TO MAKE A MOST STRONG AND VEHEMENT AQUA FORTIS

Take of the strongest aqua fortis that you can get and well rectified a pound, of mercury sublimed four ounces, and sal ammoniac two ounces. Mix all these together.

OIL OR BUTTER OF ANTIMONY IS MADE THUS

Take of crude antimony as much as you please and of sublimed mercury a like quantity. Make them both into a very fine powder and mix them and put them into a glass retort, the neck whereof must be large. Give fire by degrees in a close reverberatory, or let the distillation be made in sand. There will distill into the receiver a fatness; part whereof, sticking to the neck of the retort, will melt by a light fire being put to it. That fatness may be rectified in a retort and either be kept by itself as it is, or set in a cellar or moist place and be resolved into a liquor.

This oil must be washed in good store of water, and then there will settle to the bottom a white powder which, being washed often in fair water until all the sharpness is gone, is then called mercurius vitae, six or seven grains whereof is an excellent vomiting medicine.

A furnace for a close reverberation furnished with its retort and receiver.

A. Shows the furnace.
B. The retort.
C. The receiver.
D. The vessel filled with cold water.

HOW TO MAKE A WATER OUT OF ANTIMONY WHEREOF A FEW DROPS SHALL PURGE OR SWEAT AND WHICH HAS NEITHER SMELL OR SCARCE ANY TASTE

Take flowers of antimony and sublime them with sal ammoniac six or seven times. Then wash away the salt with warm water and dry the powder, which then lay thin on a marble in a cellar until it be dissolved (which will be in six weeks time). This water, if it be taken to the quantity of twenty drops, will purge. If in a lesser quantity, it will sweat.

TO MAKE AN OIL OR QUINTESSENCE OF METALS

Dissolve what metal or mineral you please in a strong spirit of salt (except silver which must be dissolved in aqua fortis). Draw off the phlegm in balneum, pour on rectified spirit of wine, and digest them so long until a red oil swims above which is the quintessence of metals and minerals, and is a very great secret.

THE TRUE SPIRIT OF ANTIMONY IS MADE THUS

Take of the subtle powder of the regulus of antimony as much as you please. Sublime it of itself until it will sublime no more (still putting what is sublimed to that which remains at the bottom) or with sal ammoniac six or seven times (remembering that then you must dulcify it with warm water by dissolving therewith the salt, and dry the precipitate afterwards). Set this fixed powder in a cellar, laying it very thin upon a marble stone, and in about six weeks or two months it will all be dissolved into water which must be filtered. Then evaporate part of this water, and let it stand two or three days in the cellar to crystallize. These crystals purify and dry. Mix them with three times the quantity of the gross powder of tiles, distill them in a retort, and there will come forth first a white spirit, and then a red, which you may rectify in balneum.

THE TRUE OIL OR ESSENCE OF ANTIMONY IS MADE THUS

Take of the foresaid crystals. Dissolve them in good rectified spirit of wine. Digest them two months in balneum or horse dung. Then evaporate the spirit of wine and there will remain in the bottom the true oil or essence of antimony.

Then take new crystals of antimony and let them imbibe either this oil or the foresaid spirit until they will imbibe no more. Then digest them two months in sand, and they will become a flowing fixed salt, and of excellent virtue.

The aforesaid spirit, this oil, and essence of antimony may be equalized to aurum potabile to all intents and purposes, according to a medicinal use, especially the fixed essence. The dose is five or six grains.

A BURNING SPIRIT MADE OUT OF LEAD MOST FRAGRANT AND BALSAMICAL

Take the calx of saturn, or else minium, and pour upon it so much spirit of vinegar that may cover it four fingers breadth. Digest them in a warm place the space of 24 hours, often stirring them that the matter settle not too thick in the bottom. Then decant the menstruum and pour on more. Digest it as before and this do so often until all the saltness be extracted. Filter and clarify all the menstruum being put together. Then evaporate it half away and set the other part in a cold place until it crystallizes. These crystals dissolve again in fresh spirit of vinegar. Filter and coagulate the liquor again into crystals, and this do often until they be sufficiently impregnated with the sal ammoniac of the vinegar as their proper ferment. Digest them in a temperate balneum that they may be resolved into a liquor like oil. Then distill this liquor in sand in a retort with a large receiver annexed to it, and well closed that no spirits evaporate, together with the observation of the degrees of the fire. Then there will distill forth a spirit of such a fragrant smell that the fragrancy of all flowers and compounded perfumes are not to be compared to it. After distillation when all things are cold, take out and cast away the black feces which is of no use. Then separate the yellow oil which swims on the top of the spirit and the blood red oil which sinks to the bottom of it. Separate the phlegm from the spirit in balneum. You shall by this means have a most fragrant spirit that even ravishes the senses, and so balsamical that it cures all old and new sores inward and outward, and so cordial that the dying are with admiration revived with it.

They that have this medicine need scarce use any other either for inward or outward griefs.

HOW TO TURN QUICKSILVER INTO A WATER WITHOUT MIXING ANYTHING WITH IT AND TO MAKE THEREOF A GOOD PURGATIVE AND DIAPHORETIC MEDICINE

Take an ounce of quicksilver, not purified. Put it into a bolt head of glass which you must nip up. Set it over a strong fire in sand for the space of two months, and the quicksilver will be turned into a red sparkling precipitate. Take this powder and lay it thin on a marble in a cellar for the space of two months, and it will be turned into a water which may be safely taken inwardly. It will work a little upward and downward, but chiefly by sweat.

Note that you may set diverse glasses with the same matter in the same

furnace, so that you may make the greater quantity at the time.
I suppose it is the sulphur which is in the quicksilver, and makes it so
black, that being stirred up by the heat of the fire fixes the mercury.

A FRAGRANT OIL OF MERCURY

Take of mercury seven times sublimed, and as often revived with
unslaked lime, as much as you please. Dissolve it in spirit of nitre in a
moderate heat. Then abstract the spirit of salt and edulcorate it very
well by boiling it in spirit of vinegar. Then abstract the spirit of vinegar,
and wash it again with distilled rain water. Dry it and digest it two
months in a like quantity of the best rectified spirit of wine you can get.
Distill them by retort, making your fire moderate at the beginning, and
afterwards increasing it. Then evaporate the spirit of wine in balneum,
and there will remain in the bottom a most fragrant oil of mercury.
This oil so purifies the blood by sweat and urine that it cures all
distempers that arise from the impurity thereof, as the venereal disease,
etc.

The truth is, they that have this medicine well made need but few other
medicines. The dose is four or five drops.

TO TURN MERCURY INTO A WATER BY ITSELF

Set this following vessel being made of iron into a furnace so that the
three bowls thereof be within the furnace, and the pipe and receiver be
without. Make your furnace so as that there be a great hole left open at
the top where you must put in your coals, shutting it afterwards with a
cover of stone made fit "hereunto. On top also must be holes to let in
air.

The vessel for this operation.

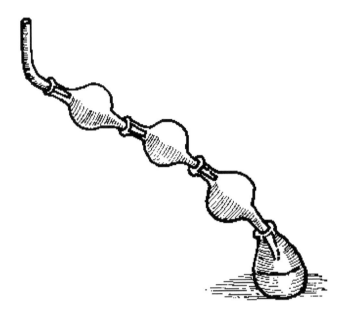

First make your iron vessel as red hot as possibly it can be made (or else you do nothing) having first annexed an earthen well glazed receiver to the bottom of it. Then put half an ounce of quicksilver at a time in at the top (which presently stop with clay) and presently the mercury will come over, part in a sharp liquor and part as crude a mercury as before, which you may put in again until it be all turned to water.

Note that unless the quicksilver gives a great crack presently after it is put in, it is a sign that the vessel is not hot enough.

This operation being well prosecuted may produce a medicine with which none under the Philosophers Elixir may compare.

How to distill spirits and oils out of minerals, vegetables, bones, horns and faster and in a greater quantity in one hour than in the common way in twenty-four.

This must be done in such a furnace as this.

A. Signifies the furnace with its iron or earthen distilling vessel walled in, to which a very large recipient is joined.

B. The distiller who with his left hand takes off the cover and with his right casts in his prepared matter with an iron ladel.

C. The form of the distilling vessel.

D. The same as it appears inward.

E. The form of the vessel not walled in but standing on the coals for other uses.

This furnace must be twice so high, as wide, and the pipe must be a foot long out of the furnace.

The vessel walled in must be of earth for the distilling of antimony, sulphur, and such things as will corrode iron; but for other things, iron is most convenient.

Before you make any distillation, let the vessel which is walled in be red hot. Then little by little cast in your matter which must be cut or powdered small, and clap down the cover into the false bottom above which is full of molten lead and, therefore, suffers no fume to go forth. When you see the fumes in the receiver (which must be of glass) to cease and condensed into a liquor, then put in more matter.

By this way you may make a far greater dispatch and distill a greater quantity out of the same proportion of matter than by the common way.

By this way there is no danger of breaking your receiver, and you may end and begin when you please, and try diverse experiments in one hour. You cannot make the fire too strong, and may make the spirits of such things as can hardly or not so well be made by a retort, as the spirits of salt, of tartar, harts horn, antimony, etc., etc.

Salt and such things as will flow must have bole or powder of brick mixed with them before they be cast into the vessel. Or, if you please, you may first dissolve what salt you please and with red hot gross powder of brick, imbibe the water. Then cast in this powder by little and little into the distilling vessel, and the salt by this means will yield its spirit quickly and in abundance. By either of these two ways you may make a pound of the spirit of nitre in an hour, and of salt in two hours. Now, whereas some things yield a spirit and a thick and heavy oil, they may be rectified thus: viz., by putting them into a retort and distilling them in sand or ashes with a gradual heat. There will come forth the phlegm of some liquors first and then the spirit, and of other some the spirit, and then the phlegm, but of all these the heavy thick oil at last which, by distilling off, becomes far clearer than before. This may again be rectified by spirit of salt as I have showed before and, therefore, need not here repeat it.

TO MAKE AN OIL OF LAPIS CALAMINARIS

Take of lapis calaminaris powdered as much as you please. Pour on it five or six times as much of rectified spirit of salt. Shake them together continually or else it will be congealed into a hard mass which can hardly be mollified again. When no more will dissolve in frigido, put it in warm sand so long until the spirit of salt be of a high yellow colon Then pour it off and put on more until all be dissolved that will. Cast away the feces, put the solution into a glass body, and distill it in sand. About the third part of the spirit of salt comes over as insipid as common water, though the spirit were well rectified before, for the dryness of the lapis calaminaris (which is the driest of all minerals and metals except zinc) retains the spirit. After the phlegm is come over, let the glass cool, and you shall find at the bottom a thick red oil, very fat, even as olive oil, and not very corrosive. Keep it from the air, or else it turns into water.

It is of wonderful virtue for inward and outward griefs, for it has in it a pure golden sulphur.

Common sulphur mixed with this oil, and melted in a strong fire, swims like water above and is transparent.

This oil distilled in a retort with pure sand in a strong fire, yields a spirit like fire scarce to be contained in any vessel and dissolves all metals except silver, and reduces pure spirit of wine into an oil within a few days.

TO MAKE OIL OF TALC

Take of the best talc reduced into very thin flakes. Make them red hot and then quench them in the strongest lixivium that soap boilers use. Do this fifteen times and it will become as white as snow. Then powder it very small and calcine it by fumigation, by the fume of some very sharp spirit as of aqua fortis or the like. When it has been calcined for the space of a fortnight, it will become somewhat mucilaginous. Then set it in any heat of putrefaction as it is (for it has imbibed enough of the sharp spirit to moisten and ferment it) for the space of two months in a bolt head nipped up. Then evaporate the acid spirit and dulcify it with distilled rain water. After this extract what you can out of it with the best rectified spirit of wine. Pour off the solution and evaporate the spirit of wine, and at the bottom will be a most beautiful oil.

The oil is the most glorious fucus or paint in the world.

TO MAKE OIL OF TALC ANOTHER WAY

Take of the foresaid powder of talc after it has been putrified and again dulcified as much as you please. Put four times as much of the best circulated oil of camphor to it. Digest them in horse dung until all the powder be dissolved, and the oil becomes mucilaginous which will be with in two months.

This is for the same use as the former.

There is required a great deal of pains, and care, and no small cost in the preparation of these oils.

OIL IS MADE OF BOLE AMMONIAC TERRA SIGILLATA AND SUCH KIND OF CLAY EARTHS THUS

Take of either of those earths as much as you please. Break it into small pieces and put it into a retort over a naked fire for the space of 12 hours, and there will distill into the receiver (which must be large) the phlegm, then white spirits in a little quantity, yet of a grateful taste and smell.

OIL OUT OF THESE KINDS OF EARTH IIS MADE BETTER THUS

Take of either of these earths which you please, as much as you will. Pour upon it distilled rain water. Set it in some warm place for a month or more and the oiliness will separate from its body of its own accord and swim upon the water. Separate the water by a tunnel, and distill the oil with five parts of the spirit of wine well rectified. There will come forth an oil of a golden color, swimming on the spirit, which is a most excellent balsam.

SPIRIT OF UNSLAKED LIME IS MADE THUS

Take of unslaked lime as much as you please. Reduce it into a subtle powder. Imbibe it with spirit of wine most highly rectified (which must be pure from all its phlegm, or else you labor in vain) as much as it can imbibe. Draw off the spirit of wine with a gentle heat, cohobate it eight or ten times, so will the fiery virtue of the lime be fortified. Take of this levigated lime ten ounces, pure salt of tartar one ounce, the feces of tartar after the salt is extracted eleven ounces. Mix these well together and put them into a glass retort coated. See that two parts of three be empty, distill them into two receivers, the phlegm into one, the spirit into the other which must have a little of rectified spirit of wine in it to receive the spirit.

If you will separate the spirit of wine, then put fire to it, and the spirit of wine will burn away, and the spirit of the lime stay behind which is a kind of a fixed spirit.

This is a very secret for the consuming of the stone in the bladder and the curing of the gout.

OIL MADE OUT OF TILE STONES CALLED THE OIL OF PHILOSOPHERS

Take of bricks or tiles as many as you please. Break them into small pieces, make them red fire hot, and then quench them in pure old oil of olive (in which let them lie until they be cold). Then take them out and grind them very small. Let the powder be put into a glass retort, coated, a fit receiver being put thereto, and distill off the oil in a naked fire by degrees which, being distilled off, keep in a vial, close stopped.
This oil is wonderful penetrating and is good against all cold distempers whatsoever.

THE LIQUOR OR WATER OF CORAL IS MADE THUS

Take sal ammoniac well purified by sublimation, of red coral finely powdered, of each a like quantity. Sublime them so often until the coral will no more rise up. Then take the calx of coral that remains in the bottom of the sublimatory, and put it on a marble or glass in the cellar to be dissolved. That which will not be dissolved, sublime again, and do as before until all be dissolved. So you have the liquor of coral.

Note that if you will have the true tincture of coral, evaporate the humidity of the foresaid liquor. Then extract the tincture out of the powder with spirit of wine, which spirit evaporate to the consistency of honey. And you have a most rare medicine.

This medicine strengthens all the parts in the body and cures all distempers that arise from the weakness thereof.

TO MAKE A WATER OUT OF LAPIS ARMENUS THAT SHALL HAVE NEITHER TASTE NOR SMELL A FEW DROPS WHEREOF SHALL PURGE

Take of lapis armenus powdered small and calcined as much as you please. Sublime it with sal ammoniac until it will sublime no more, but remain in the bottom of the sublimatory. Then take it out and lay it very thin upon a marble in a cellar, and there let it lay two months, and it will be almost all dissolved into a liquor.

Or thus:- Take of lapis armenus powdered small and calcined as much as you please. Pour upon it of distilled vinegar as much as will cover it four fingers breadth. Then set it over a gentle heat, stirring of it two or three times in an hour, for the space of six hours or thereabouts. Then the spirit being tinged very blue with the powder, filter off from the feces. Then pour more spirit of vinegar on the feces and do as before until the spirit be tinged no more. Then take all the blue spirit and vapor it away, and at the bottom you shall have a salt which you must put into a calcining pot and calcine so long in the fire until no more vapor will arise and it becomes a dark red powder. Then put it upon a marble in the cellar for the space of two months and it will be dissolved into a liquor, a few drops whereof put into a glass of beer will purge delicately.

HOW TO MAKE A FURNACE THAT SHALL OF ITSELF WITHOUT ANY VESSELS WHICH SHOULD CONTAIN THE MATTER BEING PUT INTO IT SUBLIME MINERALS AND DISTILL ALL MANNER OF OILS AND SPIRITS OUT OF MINERALS, VEGETABLES, AND ANIMALS AND THAT IN A VERY GREAT QUANTITY IN A VERY SHORT TIME AND WITH SMALL COST

The furnace is made as follows. It may be made of one piece by a potter or of brick, round or four-square, greater or lesser as you please. If the inside be one span broad in the middle, it must be high, one for the ash hole, another above the grate to the middle coal hole and two above the pipe. This pipe, being made of earth or iron, must be a span long between the furnace and the receiver, and a third part as wide as the furnace within.

The recipients must be made of glass or very good earth well luted together, the greater the better.

The First Figure

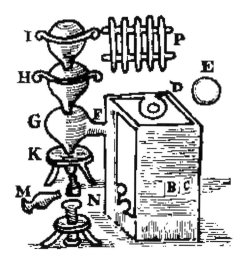

The Second Figure

A. Signifies the ash hole which must be as wide as the furnace and always open that the fire may burn the stronger.

B The middle hole of the furnace for the putting in of coals.

C. The stopple made of stone.

D. The upper hole of the furnace with a false bottom wherein sand lies which is there lain that the cover may lie the closer and keep in the fumes the better.

E. The cover which must be presently clapped on as soon as the matter to be distilled is put in.

F. The pipe which goes out of the furnace and to which the receiver is fitted.

G. The first recipient for flowers.

H. The second.

I. The third.

K. A stool whereon the first recipient rests, in the midst whereof is a hole, through which goes the neck of the recipient to which another glass is fitted.

L. The glass fitted to the recipient for the uniting the spirits that drop down.

M. Another recipient united to the former glass and into which the united spirits do run.

N. A stool through the middle of which goes a screw for the raising of that glass, which is set under the first recipient, higher or lower.

P. The grate with two thick iron bars which lie fast, upon which four or five thinner are laid which may be stirred when the furnace is made clean.

Thus far the first of the figures is explained, by which you may see how sublimation and distillation are made at one time, viz., of those things which will yield both flowers and spirits (the flowers sticking in the three upper recipients and the spirits dropping down into the lower). Now follows the explanations of the second figure which is the same with the former in respect to the furnace itself, but differing in respect of the recipients which serve for the receiving of the spirits and oils of such things as yield no flowers. Therefore I shall begin with the explanation of the receivers.

G. The first crooked pipe as it is fitted to the pipe that comes out of the furnace.
H. The recipient with its cover in which is one hole for one crooked pipe to go through, as you may see in the first H, and two holes for two pipes to go through, as you may see in the second H, and in HH.
Note that these pipes may either be fastened to the cover, being all of one piece, or they must be well luted, that no vapors may pass through. Now you must conceive that in the lower receivers the vapor that goes out of the first pipe goes first into the receiver, then out of that into the next pipe and so forward until it comes into the last receiver, by which means it is much cooled (for indeed such vapors that come out of the furnace, especially when some materials are distilled, if there were not some such art to cool them would break all recipients).
I. A tub of water wherein the recipient stands to cool the vapors and condense them.
K. The first crooked pipe as it goes into the recipient.L. The second crooked pipe, whereof one end goes into one receiver, and another end into another.
M. The last crooked pipe to which you must annex a receiver.

Now the manner of distilling is thus. Let the furnace be full of coals well kindled, then cast on your matter, and stop your furnace close. This furnace needs no retort or other vessels to be set into it. Neither can you do any hurt by too much or too little fire, and you may finish your operation when you please and in one hour try diverse experiments. It saves very much time and cost, and in one hour will do as much as can be done in another furnace in twenty-four. In one hour you may make a pound of spirit of salt with four or five pounds of coals, and as much flowers of antimony in a like space of time, and with as few coals.

If your materials be vegetables, or horn, or bones, cut them small. If hard minerals, let them be powdered very small. If salts, let them be first dissolved in water, which water must be imbibed with red hot coals until all the liquor be imbibed. Then cast in those coals into the furnace.

If you would by this means procure the spirit of hard minerals, as of antimony, and you must take them as they come from the mine, before they have passed the fire.

By this furnace you may make the spirits of such things which will not yield them in any other way.

Note that such oils and spirits as are drawn by this furnace must be rectified in spirit of salt, as I have shown.

ROS VITRIOLI IS MADE THUS

Take of the best Dansick vitriol, as much as you please, uncalcined. Put it into a glass gourd and distill it in the sand, and there will come over a water somewhat sharpish.

This water, or ros, is of greater use than the spirit or oil thereof.
It helps all inward inflammations, as of the liver, kidneys, stomach, helps the ebullition of blood, and all distempers that come from thence. This is that phlegm which most vapor away, but it is because they know not the virtues thereof.

A SWEET GREEN OIL OF VITRIOL IS MADE THUS

Take as many copporas stones as you please. Beat them small and lay them in a cool cellar. In twenty or thirty days they will attract the air and look black, and after fourteen days become whitish and sweetish. Then dissolve them in distilled rain water, then filter and evaporate the water, and they will shoot into green crystals which you may dissolve in a cellar per deliquium, being first beaten small and lain on a marble stone.

This liquor is that famous medicine of Paracelsus for the falling sickness, a few drops thereof being taken in any appropriate liquor. Take heed that it comes at no strong fire, for then, says Paracelsus, it loses its greeness and, as much as it loses of that, so much also of its virtue.

A spirit may be drawn from hence by an ingenious artist that will smell like musk or amber.

THE SULPHUR OF VITRIOL MAY WITH SPIRIT OF WINE BE EXTRACTED THUS

Take of the best Dansick vitriol half a pound and dry it by a gentle fire until it be whitish. Then pour on it of the best rectified spirit of wine thirty ounces (note that there must come to it no other moisture than the spirit of wine, and the glass also must be very dry, else you labor in vain). Then digest it in horse dung the space of a month. Then decant from the feces the spirit of wine without any troubling of it. Then in balneum evaporate the spirit, and at the bottom you will have a yellow liquor of a most wonderful slipticity.

This liquor is a famous anodynum, suppressing all noxious vapors whatsoever and causing rest.

A few drops thereof may be taken in any specifical liquor.

A SUDORIFIC WATER TO BE USED OUTWARDLY

Take of sublimed mercury very finely powdered an ounce and a half, of euphorbium powdered a scruple, spirit of wine well rectified, and rose water, of each a pound. Digest them two or three hours in a gentle balneum, the neck of the vessel which must be very long being well stopped. Then let them boil a quarter of an hour. When the liquor is cold, pour it from the feces and keep it in a glass.

If the backbone be bathed with the water, or the wrist of those that be weak, it causes sweat presently, if it be done in the bed. By which means diseases that require sweat may be cured. Also, any pained place by being bathed with this water is in a little time eased.

Note that you must not bathe any place above three or four times with it, for by being too often used it contracts the skin.

HOW TO RECTIFY OILS AND SPIRITS OF MINERALS

Put the liquor that is distilled from minerals into the retort to which give fire by degrees. The spirit will rise up into the upper receiver and the heavy oil will go into the middle receiver which is the biggest of all. Into the little receiver, annexed to the end of the middle, will pass some of the spirit which, though it passes into the middle receiver, will not stay there, but goes beyond it because it finds vent.

BOOK IV

OF ANIMALS

WATERS, SPIRITS, AND OILS, SIMPLE AND COMPOUND OUT OF ANIMALS

OIL AND WATER OUT OF BLOOD IS MADE THUS

Take of blood as much as you please. Let it stand in putrefaction in a glass vessel close covered the space of forty days. Then distill it in ashes, and there will come forth a water and oil. Extract the salt out of the feces with the said water. Calcine the salt in a crucible and then dissolve it in the said water. Then distill off the water (which will be a good rectifying of the water) and dry the salt very well, which then mix with the foresaid oil being first rectified, and digest them both together for the space of a month.

TO MAKE THE MAGISTERY OF BLOOD

Take of the purest blood as much as you please. Put it into a pelican, so that three parts of four may be empty, and then digest it a month in horse dung (in which time it will swell and become as much more as it was when it was put in). Then distill off the phlegm in balneum, and in the bottom will remain the magistery of blood which must be distilled and cohobated nine times in a retort in ashes, and then it is perfected. This magistery is of excellent virtue which, being taken inwardly, and applied outwardly cures most diseases and eases pain, being very balsamical.

ELIXIR OF MUMMY IS MADE THUS

Take of mummy (viz., of man's flesh hardened), cut small four ounces, spirit of wine terebinthinated ten ounces, and put them into a glazed vessel (three parts of four being empty) which set in horse dung to digest for the space of a month. Then take it out and express it, and let the expression be circulated a month. Then let it run through manica hippocratis, and then evaporate the spirit until that which remains in the bottom be like an oil which is the true elixir of mummy.

This elixir is a wonderful preservative against all infections, also very balsamical.

THE ESSENCE OF MAN'S BRAINS

Take the brains of a young man that has died a violent death, together with the membranes, arteries, veins, nerves, all the pith of the back, and bruise these in a stone mortar until they become a kind of pap. Then put as much of the spirit of wine as will cover it three or four fingers breadth. Then put it into a large glass so that three parts of four be empty, being hermetically closed. Then digest it half a year in horse dung. Then take it out and distill it in balneum and cohobate the water until the greatest part of the brains be distilled off.

A scruple or two of this essence taken in some specifical water once in a day is a most infallible medicine against the falling sickness.

A FAMOUS SPIRIT MADE OUT OF CRANIUM HUMANUM

Take of cranium humanum as much as you please. Break it into small pieces, which put into a glass retort well luted, with a large receiver well luted. Then put a strong fire to it by degrees, continuing of it until you see no more fumes come forth, and you shall have a yellowish spirit, a red oil, and a volatile salt.

Take this salt and the yellow spirit, and digest them by circulation two or three months in balneum, and you shall have a most excellent spirit. This spirit is of affinity with, if not the same as, that famous spirit of Dr. Goddards in Holborne.

It helps the falling sickness, gout, dropsie, infirm stomach, and indeed strengthens all weak parts, and opens all obstructions, and is a kind of panacea.

ANOTHER EXCELLENT SPIRIT MADE OUT OF CRANIUM, HARTS HORN, OR IVORY

Take of either of these. (If you take cranium, it need not be bruised at all, only broken into little pieces; if harts horn or ivory, you must cut them in thin pieces). Lay it piece by piece upon a net spread upon any vessel, being most full of water. Cover this net with another vessel very close. Then make the water boil, and keep it boiling three days and three nights, and in that time the bones or horns will be as soft as cheese. Then pound them, and to every pound thereof, put half a pound of hungarian vitriol uncalcined, and as much spirit of wine as will make them into a thin paste. This paste digest in a vessel hermetically sealed the space of a month in balneum. Then distill it in a retort in sand until all be dry, and you shall have a most excellent spirit.

This spirit is of wonderful use in the epilepsy convulsions, all fevers putrid or pestilential, passions of the heart, and is a very excellent sudorific.

This spirit may be taken from the quantity of half an ounce to an ounce in some specifical liquor.

A WATER AND OIL MADE OUT OF HAIR

Fill an earthen retort with hair cut small. Set it over the fire and fit a receiver to it. There will come over a very stinking water and oil.

This water and oil is used in Germany to be sprinkled upon fences and hedges to keep wild and hurtful cattle from coming to do harm in any place, for such is the stink of this liquor that it does frighten them from coming to any place near it.

WATER OF MILK IS MADE THUS

Take of what milk you please a gallon. In it dissolve half a pound of salt, and put to it two handfuls of plantain, and an ounce of licorice sliced. Then distill it in a hot still with a gentle fire.

This water is of excellent use in hot distempers of the lungs and kidneys.

You may put in other ingredients according to the use you would have it for.

AN EXCELLENT COMPOUND WATER OF MILK FOR ANY INFLAMMATIONS IN THE EYES

Take of woman's milk a pint, of white copperas a pound, and distill them in ashes. Note that as soon as you perceive any sharp spirit to come off, then cease.

Let inflamed eyes be washed three or four times in a day with this water, and it helps them wonderfully.

SPIRIT OF URINE IS MADE THUS

Take of the urine of a young man drinking much wine, as much as you please. Let it stand in glass vessels in putrefaction forty days. Then pouring it from its feces, distill it in a glass gourd in sand until all be dry. Then cohobate the said spirit on the caput mortuary three times. Then distill it in a gourd of a long neck and there will ascend, besides the spirit, a crystalline salt which you may either keep by itself, being called the volatile salt of urine, or mix it with its spirit which will thereby become very penetrating if they be digested for some days together.

Note that the pipe of the head must be wide or else the volatile salt will soon stop it.

Note that this salt is so penetrating that it penetrates the body of the glass.

This spirit by rectification may be made so pure and subtle that it will burn as fire and dissolve gold and precious stones.

This being often applied to any place pained with the gout eases it presently. It also quickens any part that is benumbed.

The salt volatile is Helmont's famous medicine for the jaundice.

A COMPOUND SPIRIT OF URINE

Take of hungarian vitriol a pound, and the urine of a boy that is healthy four pounds. Put these into a glass vessel well closed so that three parts of four may be empty. Digest them in balneum for the space of a month and then distill them in ashes until all be dry.

This spirit is of great virtue in the epilepsy, gout, dropsy, convulsions, being taken from two drams to half an ounce in some specifical liquor.

TO MAKE A SPIRIT OF HONEY

Take good strong stale mead, otherwise called metheglin, as much as you please, distill it in a copper still or alembic, with its refrigeratory, and it will yield a spirit like aqua vitae.

THE QUINTESSENCE OF HONEY IS MADE THUS

Take of the purest honey two pounds, and of fountain water one pound. Boil these together until the water be boiled away, taking off the scum that rises. Then take the honey and put it into a glass, four parts of five being empty. Close it well and set it in digestion a whole year and you shall have the essence of honey swimming on the top in form of an oil, being of as fragrant smell as anything in the world. The phlegm will be in the middle, and the feculent matter in the bottom, of a dark color and stinking smell.

SOME MAKE THE QUINTESSENCE OF HONEY AFTER THIS MANNER

Take as much honey as you please, of the best, and put it into a glass. First distill off the phlegm in balneum, and then extract the tincture out of what remains with the said water. Then calcine the remaining feces and extract from thence the salt with the foresaid water being distilled off from the tincture. Calcine the salt and melt it in a crucible. Then let it dissolve in a cellar, and then again evaporate it away. You shall have a most white salt which let imbibe as much of the tincture as it will. Digest them for three months, and you shall have an essence of honey.

AN ESSENCE OF HONEY MAY BE MADE THUS

Take of honey well despumated as much as you please. Pour upon it as much of the best rectified spirit of wine as will cover it five or six fingers breadth. Digest them in a glass vessel well closed (the fourth part only being full) in a temperate balneum the space of a fortnight or until the spirit be very well tinged. Then decant off the spirit and put on more until all the tincture be extracted. Put all these tinctures together, and evaporate the spirit until what remains begins to be thickish at the bottom and of a golden colon

This is a very excellent essence of honey and is of so pleasant an odor that scarce anything is like to it.

It is so cordial that it even revives the dying if two or three drops thereof be taken in some cordial water.

A MOST STRONG SPIRIT OF THE VINEGAR OF HONEY

Take a pound of honey and put to it of the best white wine vinegar six pints, an ounce of white pepper bruised small, of the strongest mustard seed bruised three ounces. Put these into a glass vessel so that three parts of four be empty. Digest them in a temperate balneum, or set the vessel in the sun for the space of a fortnight. Then distill them in balneum and you shall have a spirit far sharper than the common spirit of vinegar.

This spirit is stronger and better than any common distilled vinegar for the dissolving of hard things and extracting of the tinctures out of things.

OIL OR QUINTESSENCE OF WAX

Take of the best wax a pound and as much of pure sand well washed from all its impurity and again dried. First, melt the wax, and then mix the sand with it very exactly. Then put them into a glass retort well coated. Fit a strong receiver to it and set it in sand. Give it fire by degrees, continuing it four days, which at last must be very strong. There will come off a spiritous oil which must be rectified seven times in a glass retort, every time changing the retort, and you shall have a subtle oil of a golden color.

This oil extracts the virtues of all flowers presently, being set in the sun. It is wonderful balsamical for the cure of wounds or ulcers both inward and outward. Being applied outwardly, it also eases all pains, quickens any deadened member, as in the palsy.

WATER IS MADE OUT OF FLESH THUS

Take what flesh you please, the bloodiest part thereof, unwashed, being cut very small, and then bruised (or if it be a feathered fowl, take it being chased up and down until it be wearied, and then suddenly strangled, the feathers being plucked off without putting of it into water, and thus being plucked bare and the bowels taken out, cut the flesh, bones, gizard, liver, heart). Pour upon it as much water as will be sufficient, with what spices and herbs you please. Then set it over a gentle fire in an earthen vessel, glazed, the space of 24 hours. Put the head upon it and lute it close, and there will distill off a comfortable restorative water.

WATER OR LIQUOR IS MADE OUT OF FLESH THUS

Take of what flesh you please, or feathered fowl prepared as before. Bruise it small, and put it into a copper vessel tinned within side, without any water being put to it. Put a cover to it and lute it close. Set it in balneum or over the vapor of seething water. If the flesh be tender, it will be turned into a clear liquor the space of twelve hours, if harder it will require a longer time. You may put in what spices or herbs you please to give it a good relish and odor. After all is done you may strain it and keep it for use, being very restorative and good for weak stomachs that cannot concoct hard meat.

If this be digested in a pelican or bolt-head a fortnight, it will be far better.

After this manner may be prepared snails, worms, and such like which are very medicinal.

A VERY EXCELLENT RESTORATIVE LIQUOR

Take of the heart, lungs, and liver of a calf, the seine parts of a fox new killed, cut them small, and put to them a quart of shell snails well scoured with salt water. Let these be put into a copper vessel tinned within side and covered close that no vapor comes forth. Set this vessel over the vapor of seething water, and in 24 hours or thereabouts they will be for the most part of them turned into a liquor of themselves. Then take out this liquor and put it into a large pelican or bolt-head, putting to them a quart of old Mallago wine, rosemary flowers, betony flowers, marigold flowers, marsh wallow flowers, of each a handful; half a pound of raisins of the sun stoned, mace, and nutmeg, of each two drams; then pour off that which is clear from the feces and sweeten it with sugar or syrup of gilly flowers. Let the patient take thereof five or six spoonfuls, three or four times a day.

This liquor recovers the decaying strength wonderfully. They that by reason of their weakness can neither eat nor digest any manner of common meat will, in a short time, be sensibly strengthened if they drink a quarter of a pint of this morning and evening.

A BALSAM MADE OF BEAR'S FAT

Take of bear's fat a pound, distill it in a retort, and rectify it three or four times. To this, thus rectified, put the tincture of rosemary and made with spirit of wine, of each three ounces. Mix them well together. In these infuse cloves, cinnamon, saffron, nutmeg, of each three drams, in warm ashes the space of a night. Then strain them and put to the oil four ounces of the best wax melted and mingled well together.
This is a most incomparable balsam for the gout and palsy.

THE OIL OF SNAKES AND ADDERS

Take snakes or adders when they are fat which will be in June or July. Cut off their heads, take off their skins, and unbowel them. Put them into a glass gourd, and pour on so much of the pure spirit of wine well rectified that it may cover them four or five fingers breadth. Stop the glass well and set it in balneum until all their substance be turned into an oil, which keep well stopped for your use.

This oil does wonderful cures in recovering hearing in those that be deaf, if a few drops thereof be put warm into the ears.

A nobleman of Germany that was famous for curing the deaf used this as his chiefest medicine, by which they say he cured those that were born deaf.

THE QUINTESSENCE OF SNAKES, ADDERS, OR VIPERS

Take of the biggest and fattest snakes, adders, or vipers which you can get in June or July. Cut off their heads, take off their skins, and unbowel them. Then cut them into small pieces and put them into a glass of a wide mouth. Set them in a warm balneum so that they may be well dried which will be in three or four days. Then take them out, and put them into a bolthead. Pour on them of the best alcolized wine, as much as will cover them six or eight fingers breadth. Stop the glass hermetically, and digest them fifteen days in balneum, or so long until the wine be sufficiently covered, which pour forth. Then pour on more of the foresaid spirit of wine until all the quintessence be extracted. Then put all the tinged spirits together, and draw off the spirit in a gentle balneum, until it be thick at the bottom. On this pour spirit of wine caryophyllated, stir them well together, and digest them in a circulatory ten days. Then abstract the spirit of wine, and the quintessence remains at the bottom perfect.

This quintessence is of extraordinary virtue for the purifying of the blood, flesh, and skin and, consequently, of all diseases therein. It cures also the falling sickness, and strengthens the brain, sight, and hearing, and preserves from grey hairs, renews youth, preserves women from abortion, cures the gout, consumption, causes sweat, and is very good in and against pestilential infections.

VIPER WINE IS MADE THUS

Take of the best fat vipers, cut off their heads, take off their skins, and unbowel them. Then put them into the best canary sack, four or six according to their bigness into a gallon. Let them stand two or three months. Then draw off you wine as you drink it.

Some put them alive into the wine, and there suffocate them, and afterwards take them out, and cut off their heads, take off their skins, and unbowel them, and then put them into the same wine again, and do as before.

This wine has the same virtues as the foregoing quintessence. It also provokes to venery, cures the leprosy and such like corruptions of the blood.

KUNRATH'S FAMOUS WATER CALLED AQUA MAGNANIMITATIS

Take of pismires or ants (the biggest that have a sourish smell are the best) two handfuls, spirit of wine a gallon. Digest them in a glass vessel close shut the space of a month in which time they will be dissolved into a liquor. Then distill them in balneum until all be dry. Then put the same quantity of ants as before. Digest and distill them in the said liquor as before. Do this three times, and then aromatize the spirit with some cinnamon.

Note that upon the spirit will float an oil which must be separated. This spirit is of excellent use to stir up the animal spirit - in so much that John Casmire, Palse-grave of the Rhene and Seyfrie of Collen, General against the Turks, did always drink of it when they went to fight, to increase magnanimity and courage which it did even to admiration.

This spirit does also wonderfully irritate them that are slothful to venery.

It also provokes urine even to admiration.

It does also wonderfully irritate the spirits that are dulled and deeded with any cold distemper.

This oil does the same effects, and indeed more powerfully.

This oil does, besides what is spoken of the spirit, help deafness exceedingly, two or three drops being dropped into the ear, after it is well syringed, once in a day for a week together.

It helps also the eyes that have any film growing on them, being now and then dropped into them.

ANOTHER AQUA MAGNANIMITATIS IS MADE THUS

Take of ants or pismires a handful, of their eggs two hundred, of millepedes or woodlice one hundred, and of bees one hundred and fifty. Digest all these in two pints of spirit of wine, being very well impregnated with the brightest soot. Digest them together the space of a month, then pour off the clear spirit and keep it safe.

This water, or spirit, is of the same virtue as the former.

WATER OF DUNG IS MADE THUS

Take of any dung as much as you please. While it is still fresh, put it into a common cold still and with a soft fire distill it off. It will be best if the bottom of the still be set over a vapor. If you would have it be stronger, cohobate the said water over its feces several times; for we see there is great virtue in dung. It makes ground fertile, and many sorts thereof are very medicinal.

A WATER OF DOVES' DUNG IS MADE THUS

Take of doves' dung as much as you please. To every pound put a pint of Rhenish wine, in which let it steep all night in a gentle balneum. Then distill it in a glass gourd in ashes. Cohobate this liquor three times. If there be any volatile salt, mix it with the water.

This water is very excellent against all obstructions of the kidneys, bladder, it helps the jaundice presently, two or three spoonfuls thereof being drunk once every morning and evening.

A WATER MADE OF HORSE DUNG

Take of the dung of a horse that is fed in the stable as much as you please. Let it stand two days out of the sun and out of the wet. To every pound of this pour a pint of white wine. Let them stand in a warm balneum a fortnight. Then distill them in a glass gourd in sand. Cohobate this three or four times. If there be any volatile salt, mix it with the water.

This water is very excellent against the bastard pleurisy, stitches, wind, obstruction of the reins, bladder, very good in a dropsy, jaundice, scurvy, etc. If three or four spoonfuls be taken every morning in the water of juniper berries, it also causes sweat.

A WATER SMELLING LIKE AMBER MADE BY PARACELSUS OUT OF COW DUNG

Take of cow dung and distill it in balneum, and the water thereof will have the smell of ambergris.

This water is very excellent in all inward inflammations.

AN EXCELLENT SUDORIFIC MADE OF THE YOUNG BUDS OF HARTSHORN

Take of the young buds of hartshorn, while they are full of blood and moist. Bruise them into a paste. Then mix as much canary wine as will make a very thin paste. Distill them in ashes until they be very dry. This is an excellent sudorific in all burning fevers and epidemical diseases. If a spoonful be taken by itself or in any appropriated liquor.

OIL OUT OF BONES AND HORNS IS MADE THUS

Take of what bones you please. Reduce them to a gross powder, and put them into a retort, putting a strong fire by degrees "hereunto. There will come forth an oil and volatile salt, both which you may mix together and digest them into an essence, the oil being first rectified with spirit of wine.

THE WATER OF SWALLOWS AGAINST THE FALLING SICKNESS

Take of swallows, cut into small pieces without separating anything from them six ounces, of castoreum cut small an ounce. Mix them together, and infuse them twelve hours in half a pint of canary wine. Then put them into a glass gourd and distill them in sand until all be dry. Then cohobate the liquor three times.

This water, being drunk to the quantity of two spoonfuls every morning, cures them that have the falling sickness.

OIL OF EGGS IS MADE THUS

Take of the yolks of eggs boiled very hard. Rub them in pieces with your fingers. Then fry them in a pan over a gentle fire, continually stirring them with a spoon until they become red, and the oil be resolved and flow from them. Then put them into a hair cloth, and so press forth the oil.

This oil cleans the skin from any filthiness contracted by heat. It cures pustules, chaps, excoriations, ring worm, and especially all burnings.

A WATER OF THE WHITES OF EGGS THAT WILL CURE A WOUND WITHOUT ANY VISIBLE SCAR

Take as many eggs as you please and boil them very hard. Then cut them in the middle and take out the yolks, filling up the cavities with some of those whites, being first bruised into a paste. Then put both sides of the eggs together as before, tie them together with a thread, and with a string hang them in the middle of a gourd glass, so that they touch not the sides. Stop this glass very close and set it in balneum. You shall see those whites which were bruised drop down into a liquor which you must gather up out of the bottom of the glass and keep. You will have very little of this liquor.

This liquor applied to any green wound with a feather cures it presently, wheresoever it be, without any visible scar. It cures most wonderfully all wounds in the eyes.

A WATER OF CRABS IS MADE THUS

Take of crabs or crawfish, as many as you please. Break them to pieces and macerate them in water of sengreen for the space of a day. Then distill them and cohobate the water three times.

This water is of singular virtue in all manner of inflammations inward and outward.

AN OIL OR LIQUOR IS MADE OUT OF CRAB EYES THUS

Take of crabs' eyes very finely powdered five parts, oil of tartar per deliquium six parts (this oil of tartar must be made of salt of tartar after it has flowed in the fire). Digest them in horse dung the space of a month. Then coagulate the liquor and make an extraction with the best rectified spirit of wine that can be made (or else you lose your labor). Then evaporate the spirit of wine, and there remains an oil at the bottom.

This oil is of wonderful virtue in all putrid fevers and such like distempers, and also in all obstructions, especially, of the kidneys.

WATER OF SPAWN OF FROGS IS MADE THUS

Take of the spawn of frogs gathered in March, as much as you please. Put a handful of salt to every quart, and put them into a common cold still. With a gentle fire distill off the water until no more will distill.

A COMPOUND WATER OF THE SPERM OF FROGS

Take of the sperm of frogs gathered in March about the new of the moon four pounds, of cow dung fresh six pounds. Mix them well together and let them stand the space of a day. Then distill them in ashes.

This water allays all hot pains both inward and outward, especially of the gout.

ANOTHER COMPOUND WATER OF THE SPERM OF FROGS

Take of the sperm of frogs gathered in March two pounds and a half, the urine of a young man three pints, new treakle two ounces and a half, white vitriol, salt, alum, of each four ounces. Then distill them and put to the water an ounce and a half of the salt of vitriol, camphor, and saffron, of each an ounce.

This water being applied outwardly helps all pains, especially of the gout, and such like, and also allays hot or cold swellings. It also stenches bleeding.

BOOK V

A MISCELLANY OF SPAGYRICAL EXPERIMENTS AND CURIOSITIES

THE SPAGYRICAL ANATOMY OF WATER

Water seems to be a body so very homogeneous, as if neither nature nor art could discover any heterogeneity in the parts thereof. Thus indeed it seems to the eye of the vulgar, but to that of a philosopher far otherwise, as I shall endeavor to make credible by presenting to your consideration a twofold process of the discovering of the dissimilarity of parts thereof, whereof the one is natural only, and the other artificial. But before I speak of either, it must be premised that in the element of water there is great plenty of the spirit of the world which is more predominant in it than in any other element, for the use and benefit of universal nature, and that this spirit has three distinct substances, viz. salt, sulphur, and mercury. Now, by salt we must understand a substance very dry, vital, and radical, having in it the beginning of corporification, as I may call it. By sulphur, a substance full of light and vital heat, or vivifying fire, containing in itself the beginning of motion, and by mercury we must understand a substance abounding with radical moisture, with which the sulphur of life, or vital fire, is cherished and preserved. Now, these substances which are in the spirit of the world make all fountains and waters, but with some difference, according to the predominancy of either. This several predominancy therefore is the ground of the variety of productions. I say "of productions" because all things are produced out of water. For water is both the sperm and the menstruum of the world; the former, because it includes the seed of everything; the latter, because the sperm of nature is putrefied in it, so that the seed included in it should be actuated and take upon it the diverse forms of things, and because by it the seed itself, and all things produced of seed, grow and are increased. Now, this being premised, I shall show you what the natural process is which I shall make plain by instancing in three several productions. viz. of the spawn of frogs, of stones and of vegetables.

The spawn of frogs is produced after this manner, viz. the sulphur which is in the water, being by the heat of the sun resolved and dissolved, is greedily and with delight conceived by the element of water, even as the sperm of a male is by the matrix of the female, and that upon this account. The water wants siccity which the sulphur has and, therefore exceedingly desiring it, does greedily attract it to itself. Sulphur also wants humidity and, therefore, attracts the humidity of the water. Moreover, the humidity of the water has the humidity of the salt laid up occultly in it. Also, the sulphur cherishes the humidity of the fire and desires nothing more than the humidity of the salt that is in the water. Sulphur also contains the siccity of the salt, whence it is that salt requires a siccity from the sulphur. And thus do these attractive virtues mutually act upon each other's subject. Now, by this means there is a conception made in the water which now begins to be turgid, puffed up, and troubled, as also to be grosser and more slimy, until out of the spermatic vessels the sperms be cast upward, in which sperms after a while appear black specks which are the seed of the frogs and by the heat of the sun are in a short time turned into the same, by which it appears there are dissimilar parts in water.

Stones are produced out of water that has a mucilaginous mercury which the salt, with which it abounds, fixes into stones. This you may see clearly by putting stones into water, for they will after a time contract a mucilaginous slimy matter which, being taken out of the water and set in the sun, becomes to be of a stony nature. And whence come those stones, gravel, and sand which we see in springs ? They are not washed down out of the mountains and hills (as some think) from whence the waters spring. Neither were they in the earth before the springs broke forth (as some imagine) and now appear by washing away of the earth from them. For if you dig around the springs, even beyond the heads of them, you shall find no stones at all in the earth, only in the veins thereof through which the water runs. Now, the reason of the smallness of the stones is the continual motion of the water which hinders them from being united into a continued bigness. I shall make a further confirmation of this in the artificial process of manifesting the heterogeneity of water. I shall here only add the assertion of Helmont, saying that with his alkahest all stones and, indeed, all things may be turned into water. If so, then you know what the maxim is, viz., all things may be resolved into that from whence they had their beginning. Vegetables are produced out of water, as you may clearly see by the waters sending forth plants that have no roots fixed in the bottom, of which sort is the herb called "duckweed" which puts forth a little string into the water which is as it were the root thereof. For the confirmation of this, that this herb may be produced out of mere water, there is a gentleman at this time in the city, of no small worth, that says he had fair water standing in a glass diverse years, and at last a plant sprang out of it. Also, if you put some plants, as water mint, etc., into a glass of fair water, it will germinate and shoot out into a great length, and also take root in the water, which root will in a short time be so increased and extended as to fill up the glass; but you must remember that you put fresh water into the glass once in two or three days. Hereunto, also, may be added the experiment of Helmont concerning the growth of a tree. For (says he) I took two hundred pound weight of earth dried in an oven and put it into a vessel, in which I set a willow tree which weighed five pounds which, by the addition of water to the earth, did in five years time grow to such a bigness as that it weighed 169 pounds, at which time I also dried and weighed the earth, and within two ounces it retained its former weight. Besides, the ancients have observed that some herbs have grown out of snow, being putrefied. And do not we see that all vegetables are nourished and increased with an insipid water, for what else is their juice? If you cut a vine in the month of March, it will drop diverse gallons of insipid water which water if it had remained in the trunk of the vine would in a little time have been digested into leaves, stalks, and grapes, which grapes also by a further maturation would have yielded a wine, out of which you might have extracted a burning spirit. Now, I say, although this insipid water be by the specifical sulphur and salt of the vine fixed into the stalks, leaves, and grapes of the vine, yet these give it not a corporificative matter, for that it had before, and an aptitude and potentiality to become what afterwards it proves to be. For indeed stalks, leaves, and grapes were potentially in it before, all which now it becomes to be actually by virtue of the sun and of the aforesaid sulphur and salt, whereof as I said could not add any bulk to them.

Moreover, do not we see that when things are burned and putrefied, they ascend up into the air by way of vapor and fume and then descend by way of insipid dew or rain? Now, what do all these signify but that from water are all things produced, and in it are dissimilar parts? The artificial process is this: take of what water you please, whether well water, fountain, river, or rain water, as much as you please. Let it settle three or four hours until the slime thereof separates itself. Then digest it the space of a month, after which time evaporate the fourth part by a very gentle heat and cast it away, being but the phlegm. Then distill off the remainder of the water until the feces only be left, which feces will be a slimy saltish substance. This middle substance distill again as before, casting away every time the fourth part, as phlegm, and keeping the feces by themselves for a further use, and this do seven times. Note that after the fourth or fifth distillation the water will distill over like milk, coloring the head of your still so that it can hardly be washed or scoured off. This pure water after the seventh distillation will leave no feces behind, and if you digest it three months it will be coagulated into stones and crystals which some magnify very much for the cure of inward and outward putrefactions, out of which also may be made a dissolving spirit. Note that as this water stands in digestion you may see diverse curious colors. Now, as for the feces which I spoke of (which indeed all waters, even the sweetest, leave at the bottom) being as I said a saltish slime and in taste, as it were, a medium between salt and nitre, take them and distill them in a retort in sand. There will first come forth a white fume which, being condensed, descends in a straight line to the bottom. Next will come over a red oil of great efficacy, exceeding the virtues of the spirit of salt or nitre. For confirmation of part of this process, take May dew gathered in the morning (when it has not rained the night before) and put it into a glass vessel, covered with a parchment pricked full of holes, and set it in the heat of the sun for the space of four months. There will store of green feces fall to the bottom, the residue of the water being white and clear. Now by all this you may conclude what manner of dissimilarity there is in the parts of water. I shall add but one observation more, and so conclude this subject.

Take a flint out of river water and put it into a gourd glass. Pour upon it as much river water as will fill the glass. Evaporate this water until the flint be dry. Then pour on more fresh water. Do this so long until the flint will fill up the glass (for in a little time it will fill it up and become to be of the form or figure of the glass) for it attracts to itself the mucilaginousness of the water which, indeed, is a slimy saltish matter and the true matter of stones. And thus you shall have that done by art in few days which nature would have been perfecting many years and, indeed, just such a flint as is produced in the rivers. Anyone that should see this flint in the glass would wonder how it should come in there. You may break your glass and take out your flint.

There are diverse such processes which may be used but, in effect, they may demonstrate but little more concerning the potential heterogeneity of water and, therefore, to avoid tediousness, I shall here end with the anatomy of water, concerning which if anyone can make a further illustration, let him be candid and impart it and I shall be glad to learn of him and, in the meantime, let him accept of these, my endeavors.

THE SPAGYRICAL ANATOMY OF WINE

I shall not speak here of the juice of grapes as being naturally divided into wine, tartar, and lees, but of wine as artificially divided into pure spirit, phlegm, and feces.

The spirit is that hot, subtle, pure, clear, cordial, and balsamical substance which arises with a small heat after four or five distillations, being indeed but the twentieth part of the wine. This spirit is not that inebriating substance of the wine as most think, for a man may drink the spirit that is extracted out of ten pints of wine without distempering of his brain at all when, as perhaps, he would be distempered with drinking a pint or two of the wine.

Now, this spirit contains in it a subtle ammoniac and essential sulphur inseparably conjoined which, indeed, are the life of the spirit, and may be separated from the mercurial or watery part thereof which, after separation of them, remains insipid, but yet of wonderful subtility. They may be separated thus: first, rectify the spirit as high as you can the ordinary way. Then rectify it once or twice in these following vessels.

Note that if there be any phlegm remaining in the spirit, it will go no
further than the middle receiver, especially the second time. By this
means you have so subtle a spirit that unless it is kept close stopped it
will fly away in the air. Then take of this spirit two ounces, and pour it
upon six ounces of calcined tartar before the salt be extracted, and
mingle them together. Then distill it in balneum, and there will come
over an insipid water which, as I said before, is very subtle. Then put on
a like quantity of the said spirit as before, and distill it off. This do so
long until the water that comes over is not insipid, but the spirit comes
over again hot as it was poured on. For by this time the fixed matter is
glutted with the sal ammoniac and sulphur of the spirit. Then put this
dried matter into a glass sublimatory, and put fire to it, and there will
sublime a salt from thence, even as camphor is sublimed. This salt is the
true essence of wine, indeed, and its virtues are wonderful, for there is
no disease, whether inward or outward, that can withstand it. This is

that essence of wine of the philosophers which is so penetrating, oh wonderful cordial and balsamical, which if you do once obtain, you shall need but few other medicines.

Now, this spirit or aqua vitae is in all vegetables as you may see in malt and vegetables that are putrefied before they are distilled which then yield a burning spirit. Yet it is in wine more than in any other liquors. I say liquors, for if you take eight gallons of sack and as much wheat, which is a solid body, and the wheat being malted will yield more aqua vitae than the sack.

The phlegm is that which remains after the spirit is distilled off, and is a putrid, insipid, cold, narcotic, and inebriating liquor, debilitating the stomach and offending the head. A few spoonfuls of this will presently make a man drunk, when as two pints of wine itself would hardly do it. Nay, the phlegm of half a pint of wine will make a man drunk. Whence you may collect what a great corrector of malignant spirits and vapors the spirit of wine is which, while it is mixed with the phlegm before distillation, does temper and correct this inebriating quality thereof, and as it does this, so also being given (I mean the pure dephlegmated spirit) to them that are already inebriated, does much allay their distemper. This phlegm therefore being of so narcotic a quality is the cause of palsies and such like distempers.

Moreover, it is to be observed that when this phlegm is distilled off there remains at the bottom a viscous corrosive matter which by reason of its viscosity is the cause of obstructions, and by reason of its corrosiveness the cause of the gout, colic, stone, etc.
This feces, being distilled, yields a sharp spirit and fetid oil which leave behind them a saltish substance out of which, when the salt is extracted, there remains an insipid earth.

Now, if any shall object against what I have asserted and say that aqua vitae or spirit of wine are inebriating, the causes of paley, gout, stone, colic, weak stomachs, and such like, as we see by daily experience in those that are given to the drinking of these liquors, to which I answer it is true. But then I must distinguish of aqua vitae and the spirit of wine, for there is a common aqua vitae and spirit of wine, of which also they make anise seed water by putting a few anise seeds "hereunto, and other such like waters, as clove, angelica, lemon, etc., with which this nation is most abominably cheated, and their health impaired. But these are not rectified thoroughly, but three parts of four of them are an insipid narcotic phlegm, containing in it the feces I spoke of, all which I can in a day separate from the true pure spirit, which spirit rather prevents than causes such distempers And the truth is, all the goodness of the wine is from this pure spirit.

THE FAMOUS ARCANUM OR RESTORATIVE MEDICAMENT OF PARACELSUS CALLED HIS HOMUNCULUS

First we must understand that there are three acceptions of the word "Homunculus" in Paracelsus, which are these.

1. Homunculus is a superstitious image made in the place, or name of anyone, that it may contain an astral and invisible man, wherefore it was made for a superstitious use.

2. Homunculus is taken for an artificial man, made of sperma humanum masculinum digested into the shape of a man, and then nourished and increased with the essence of man's blood; and this is not repugnant to the possibility of nature and art. But is one of the greatest wonders of God which He ever did suffer mortal man to know. I shall not here set down the full process because I think it unfit to be done, at least to be divulged. Besides neither this nor the former is for my present purpose.

3. Homunculus is taken for a most excellent arcanum or medicament extracted by the spagyrical art from the chiefest staff of the natural line in man, and according to this acception I shall here speak of it. But before I show you this process, I shall give you an account why this medicament is called homunculus, and it is this: No wise man will deny that the staff of life is the nutriment thereof, and that the chiefest nutriment is bread and wine, being ordained by God, and nature above all other things for the sustentation thereof. Besides Paracelsus preferred this nutriment for the generation of the blood and spirits, and the forming thence the sperm of his homunculus. Now, by a suitable allusion the nutriment is taken for the life of man and, especially, because it is transmuted into life. And again the life is taken for the

man, but unless a man be alive he is not a man, but the carcass only of a man, and the basest part thereof which cannot perfectly be taken for the whole man, as the noblest part may. Inasmuch, therefore, as the nutriment or aliment of life may be called the life of man, and the life of man be called man, this nutriment extracted out of bread and wine, and being by digestion exalted into the highest purity of a nutritive substance, and consequently becoming the life of man, being so potentially, may metaphorically be called homunculus.

The process which in part shall be set down allegorically is thus. Take the best wheat and the best wine, of each a like quantity. Put them into a glass which you must hermetically seal. Then let them putrefy in horse dung three days, or until the wheat begins to germinate or to sprout forth, which then must be taken forth and bruised in a mortar and be pressed through a linen cloth. There will come forth a white juice like milk. You must cast away the feces. Let this juice be put into a glass which must not be above half full. Stop it close and set it in horse dung as before for the space of fifty days. If the heat be temperate, and not exceeding the natural heat of man, the matter will be turned into a spagyrical blood and flesh, like an embryo. This is the principal and next matter out of which is generated a two-fold sperm, viz., of the father and mother generating the homunculus, without which there can be made no generation, whether human or animal.

From the blood and flesh of this embryo let the water be separated in balneum, and the air in ashes, and both be kept by themselves. Then to the feces of the latter distillation, let the water of the former distillation be added, both which must (the glass being close stopped) putrefy in balneum the space of ten days. After this, distill the water a second time (which is then the vehiculum of the fire) together with the fire, in ashes. Then distill off this water in a gentle balneum, and in the bottom remains the fire which must be distilled in ashes. Keep both these apart. And thus you have the four elements separated from the chaos of the embryo.

The feculent earth is to be reverberated in a close vessel for the space of four days. In the interim, distill off the fourth part of the first distillation in balneum and cast it away. The other three parts distill in ashes, and pour it upon the reverberated earth, and distill it in a strong fire. Cohobate it four times, and so you shall have a very clear water which you must keep by itself. Then pour the air on the same earth, and distill it in a strong fire. There will come over a clear, splendid, odoriferous water which must be kept apart. After this pour the fire upon the first water, and putrefy them together in balneum the space of three days. Then put them into a retort and distill them in sand, and there will come over a water tasting of the fire. Let this water be distilled in balneum. What distills off, keep by itself, as also what remains in the bottom which is the fire, and keep by itself. This last distilled water pour again upon its earth, and let them be macerated together in balneum for the space of three days. Then let all the water be distilled in sand, and let what will arise be separated in balneum, and the residence remaining in the bottom be reserved with the former residence. Let the water be again poured upon the earth, be abstracted and separated as before until nothing remains in the bottom which is not separated in balneum. This being done, let the water which was last separated be mixed with the residue of its fire, and be macerated in balneum three or four days, and all be distilled in balneum that can ascend with that heat. Let what remains be distilled in ashes from the fire, and what shall be elevated is aerial. And what remains in the bottom is fiery. These two last liquors are ascribed to the two first principles, the former to mercury and the latter to sulphur. They are accounted by Paracelsus not as elements but their vital parts being, as it were, the natural spirits and soul which are in them by nature. Now, both are to be rectified and reflected into their center with a circular motion, so that this mercury may be prepared with its water being kept clear and odoriferous in the upper place, but the sulphur by itself. Now, it remains that we look into the third principle. Let the reverberated earth, being ground upon a marble, imbibe its own water which did above remain after the last separation of the liquors made in balneum, so that this be the fourth part of the weight of its earth and be congealed by the heat of ashes into its earth. Let this be done so often, the proportion being observed, until the earth has drunk up all its water. And lastly, let this earth be sublimed into a white powder, as white as snow, the feces being cast away. This earth, being sublimed and freed from its obscurity, is the true chaos of the elements, for it contains those things occult, seeing it is the salt of nature in which they lie hid being, as it were, reflexed in their center. This is the third principle of Paracelsus, and the salt, which is the matrix, in which the two former sperms, viz., of the man and woman, the parents of the homunculus, viz., of mercury and sulphur are to be put, and to be closed up together in a glazed womb sealed with Hermes' seals for the true generation of the homunculus produced from the spagyrical embryo. And this is the homunculus or great arcanum, otherwise called the nutritive medicament of Paracelsus.

This homunculus or nutritive medicament is of such virtue that presently after it is taken into the body it is turned into blood and spirits. If then diseases prove mortal because they destroy the spirits, what mortal disease can withstand such a medicine that does so soon repair and so strongly fortify the spirits as this homunculus, being as the oil to the flame, into which it is immediately turned, thereby renewing the same. By this medicament, therefore, as diseases are overcome and expelled, so also youth is renewed and grey hairs prevented.

AN ARTIFICIAL WAY TO MAKE FLESH

Take of the crumbs of the best wheaten bread as soon as it comes out of the oven, being very hot, as much as you please. Put it into a glass vessel which you must presently hermetically close. Then set it in digestion in a temperate balneum the space of two months, and it will be turned into a fibrous flesh.

If any artist should please to exalt it to a higher perfection according to the rules of art, he may find out how great a nourisher and restorative wheat is, and what an excellent medicine it may make.
Note that there must be no other moisture put into the glass besides what is in the bread itself.

PARACELSUS, HIS WAY FOR THE RAISING OF A DEAD BIRD TO LIFE AND FOR THE GENERATING MANY SERPENTS OF ONE BOTH WHICH ARE PERFORMED BY PURTEFACTION

A bird is restored to life thus. Take a bird and put it alive into a gourd glass and seal it hermetically. Burn it to ashes in the third degree of fire. Then putrefy it in horse dung into a mucilaginous phlegm. So, by a continued digestion that phlegm must be brought to a further maturity (being taken out and put into an oval vessel of a just bigness to hold it) by an exact digestion, and will become a renewed bird which, says

Paracelsus, is one of the greatest wonders of nature, and shows the great virtue of putrefaction.

Cut a serpent into small pieces, which put into a gourd glass and hermetically seal. Then putrefy them in horse dung, and the whole serpent will become living again in the glass either in the form of worms or spawn of fishes. Now, if these worms be in a fitting manner brought out of putrefaction and nourished, many hundred serpents will be bred out of one serpent, whereof every one will be as big as the first. And as it is said of the serpent, so also many other living creatures may be raised and restored again.

TO MAKE AN ARTIFICIAL MALLAGO WINE

First, take a wine barrel well trooped and dressed, with one end being open, to which a close cover must be well fitted, which must be to take off and put on at pleasure. Set it in a warm place winter or summer, and fill it full with clear and pure water, to each three gallons. Put six pounds of the best mallago raisins which you must bruise in a stone mortar. Then strong upon the water, upon each twenty gallons of which you must cast a handful of calx vive. Then cover the vessel close with the cover, and cast clothes upon it to keep it warm. Let it stand four or five days to work as wine or beer do when they be new. Then see if the raisins be risen up to the top of the water. If so, then put them down again and cover it as before. Let them thus stand three weeks or a month together, the raisins being every fourth or fifth day put down in case they rise up. Then put a tap into the vessel three or four fingers above the bottom and try if it be good and taste like wine. If not, let it stand a while longer; but if so, draw it off into another wine vessel, and to every twenty gallons that you have drawn off, put a pint of the best aqua vitae, two new laid hens eggs, and a quart of alligant beaten well together. Let it stand in a cellar as other wine does until it be clear and fit to be drunk.

TO MAKE AN ARTIFICIAL CLARET WINE

Take six gallons of water, two gallons of the best cider, and put "hereunto eight pounds of the best mallago raisins bruised in a mortar. Let them stand close covered in a warm place the space of a fortnight, every two days stirring them well together. Then press out the raisins and put the liquor into the said vessel again, to which add a quart of the juice of raspberries, and a pint of the juice of black cherries. Cover this liquor with bread spread thick with strong mustard, the mustard side being downward, and so let it work by the fireside three or four days. Then turn it up and let it stand a week, and then bottle it up. And it will taste as quick as bottle beer and, indeed, become a very pleasant drink and, indeed, far better and wholesomer than our common claret.

AN ARTIFICIAL MALMESEY

Take two gallons of english honey and put it into eight gallons of the best spring water. Set these in a vessel over a gentle fire. When they have boiled gently an hour take them off, and when they be cold put them into a small barrel or runlet, hanging in the vessel a bag of spices. Set it in the cellar, and in half a year you may drink thereof.

TO MAKE AN EXCELLENT AROMATICAL HYPPOCRAS

Take of cinnamon two ounces, ginger an ounce, cloves and nutmeg of each two drams, of white pepper half a dram, of cardamum two drams, and of musk mallowseed three ounces. Let all these be bruised and put into a bag and hung in six gallons of wine. Note that you must put a weight in the bag to make it sink.

Some boil these spices in wine which they then sweeten with sugar, and then let run through a hyppocras bag and afterwards bottle it up and use when they please.

A Single Hyppocras Bag, or Manica Hippocratis

When you would have this or any other liquor to be very clear, you may use the triple hyppocras bag, for what feces pass the first will stay in the second, and what in the second will stay in the last. Note that these bags must be made of white cotton.

A triple hyppocras bag is only one hung above another after this manner.

TO MAKE EXCELLENT HYPPOCRAS WINE IN AN INSTANT

Take of cinnamon two ounces, nutmeg, ginger, of each half an ounce, cloves two drams. Bruise these small, and then mix them with as much spirit of wine as will make them into a paste. Let them stand close covered in a glass the space of six days in a cold place. Then press out the liquor and keep it in a glass.

A few drops of this liquor put into any wine gives it a gallant relish and odor, and makes it as good as any hyppocras whatsoever and that in an instant.

Note that if the wine be of itself harsh, it will not be amiss to sweeten it with sugar, for thereby it is made far more grateful.

This also being put into beer will make it very pleasant and aromatical.

ANOTHER WAY TO MAKE HYPPOCRAS OR MAKE ANY WINE TO TASTE OF ANY VEGETABLE IN AN INSTANT

Take what wine you please, and according as you would have it taste of this or that spice or any other vegetable, of one or more together, you may drop a few drops of the distilled oil of the said spices or vegetables into the wine, and brew well together and you may make in an instant all sorts of hyppocras or other wines. As for example, if you would have wormwood wine, two or three drops of oil of wormwood put into a good Rhenish wine, being well brewed together, will make a wormwood wine exceeding any that you shall meet withall in the Rhenish wine houses.

TO MAKE A GOOD RASPBERRY WINE

Take a gallon of sack in which let two gallons of raspberries stand, steeping the space of 24 hours. Then strain them and put to the liquor three pounds of raisins of the sun stoned. Let them stand together four or five days, being sometimes stirred together. Then pour off the clearest and put it up in bottles and set it in a cold place. If it be not sweet enough you may add some sugar to it.

TWO OTHER WAYS TO MAKE IT ALL THE YEAR AT AN INSTANT

Take of the juice of raspberries and put it into a bottle which you must stop close. Set it in a cellar. It will become clear, and keep all the year, and become very fragrant.

A few spoonfuls of this put into a pint of wine sweetened well with sugar gives it an excellent and full taste of the raspberries.

If you put two or three ounces of the syrup of raspberries to a pint of wine it will do as well, but then you need use no other sugar, for that will sweeten it sufficiently.

TO MAKE MEAD OR METHEGLIN THAT IT SHALL TASTE STALE AND QUICK WITHIN A FORTNIGHT AND BE FIT TO DRINK

To every three gallons of water put one gallon of the purest honey. Put what herbs and spices you please. Boil it and skim it well, now and then putting in some water. When it is sufficiently boiled, take it off, and when it is almost cold, put it into a wooden vessel. Set it by the fireside, and cover it over with bread spread thick with the strongest mustard, the mustard side being downwards. So let it stand three days, and it will work. Only put a cloth over it. Then turn it up, and after a week draw it forth into bottles and set it into a cellar. After another week you may drink of it, for it will taste as quick as bottle beer that is a fortnight old and, indeed, as stale as other mead will in half a year.

TO MAKE A SPIRIT OF AMBERGRIS THAT A FEW DROPS THEREOF SHALL PERFUME A PINT OF WINE MOST RICHLY

Take of ambergris two drams, and of musk a dram. Cut them small and put them into a pint of the best rectified spirit of wine. Close up the glass hermetically and digest them in a very gentle heat until you perceive they are dissolved. Then you may make use of it.

Two or three drops or more if you please of this spirit, put into a pint

of wine. gives it a rich odor.
Or if you put two or three drops around the brim of a glass, it will do
as well.

Half a spoonful of it taken either of itself or mixed with some specifical
liquor is a most rich cordial.

AN EXCELLENT SWEET WATER

Take a quart of orange flower water, as much rose water, and add
thereto of musk-mallow seeds grossly bruised four ounces, of benjamin
two ounces, of storax an ounce, of labdanum six drams, of lavender
flowers two pugills, of sweet marjoram as much, of calimus aromaticus
a dram. Distill all these in a glass still in balneum, the vessels being very
well closed so that no vapor breathes forth.

Note that you may make a sweet water in an instant by putting a few
drops of some distilled oils together into some rose water and brewing
them well together.

TO PURIFY AND TO GIVE AN EXCELLENT SMELL AND
TASTE UNTO OIL OF OLIVE THAT THEY THAT LOATHE
IT MAY DELIGHT TO EAT IT

Take of a good sort of oil of olive, though not of the best. Put the same
into a vessel of earth or copper that has a little hole in the bottom
thereof which you may stop with wax or a cork to open at your
pleasure. In this vessel, for every quart of oil add four quarts of fair
water, and with a wooden spatula or spoon beat them well together for
a quarter of an hour's space. When you have so done, open the hole in
the bottom and let out the water, for the oil does naturally flee above,
as being the lighter body. As soon as the water is passed away, stop the
hole, and put in other cold water. Begin a new agitation as before, and
work in the like manner diverse times as you did at the first, until in the
end the oil be well cleansed and clarified. If the last time you work it
with rose water, it will be so much the better. Then hang in the midst
of the oil a coarse bag full of nutmeg sliced, cloves bruised, and the
rinds of oranges and lemons cut small. Set the vessel in balneum for two

or three hours and, I suppose, he that loathes oil will be easily by this means drawn to a liking of it.

ANOTHER WAY

Set oil of olive in the sun in summertime until there settles a good store of soul and gross lees, from the which by declination pour out the clear oil. Keep it until the next winter, and after the same has been congealed with some frosty weather the oil will be most sweet and delectable to taste.

After this manner you may clarify all thick oils and all kinds of grease but, then, you must use warm water instead of cold.

TO PURIFY BUTTER THAT IT SHALL KEEP FRESH AND SWEET A LONG TIME AND BE MOST WONDERFUL SWEET IN TASTE

Dissolve butter in a clean glazed or silver vessel and in a pan or kettle of water with a slow and gentle fire. Then pour the same so dissolved into a basin that has some. fair water therein. When it is cold, take away the curds and the whey that remains in the bottom. And if you will be at the charge thereof, you may the second time (for it must be twice dissolved) dissolve the butter in rose water, working them well together. The butter thus clarified will be as sweet in taste as the marrow of any beast, by reason of the great impurity that is removed by this manner of handling, the first part thereof being drosse which makes the butter many times offensive to the stomach.

TO MAKE BUTTER TASTE OF ANY VEGETABLE WITHOUT ALTERING THE COLOR THEREOF

When the butter is taken out of the churn and well worked from the ferous part thereof, mix with the said butter as much of the oil of that vegetable which you like best until the same be strong enough in taste to your liking. Then temper them well together.

If you do in the month of May mix some oil of sage with your butter, it may excuse you from eating sage with your butter.

If you mix the oil with the aforesaid clarified butter, it will be far better and serve for a most dainty dish and, indeed, a great rarity.

TO MAKE CHEESE TASTE STRONG OF ANY VEGETABLE WITHOUT DISCOLORING OF IT

You may mix the distilled oil of what vegetable you would have the cheese taste of with the curd before the whey be pressed out. But be sure you mix them very well that all places may taste alike of it. You may make it taste stronger or weaker of it, as you please, by putting in more or less of the oil.

TO PURIFY AND REFINE SUGAR

Make a strong lixivium of calx vive, wherein dissolve as much coarse sugar as the lixivium will bear. Then put in the white of eggs (of two to every quart of the liquor) being beaten into an oil. Stir them well together and let them boil a little, and there will arise a scum which must be taken off as long as any will arise. Then pour all the liquor through a great woolen cloth bag, and so the feces will remain behind in the bag. Then boil the liquor again so long until some drops of it being put upon a cold plate will, when they be cold, be congealed as hard as salt. Then pour out the liquor into pots or moulds made for that purpose, having a hole in the narrower end thereof which must be stopped for one night after, and after that night be opened. There will a moist substance drop forth which is called molasses or treakle. Then with potters clay cover the ends of the pot, and as the clay sinks down by reason of the sinking of the sugar, fill them up with more clay, repeating the doing thereof until the sugar shrinks no more. Then take it out until it be hard and dried, and then bind it up in papers.

TO MAKE A VEGETABLE GROW AND BECOME MORE GLORIOUS THAN ANY OF ITS SPECIES

Reduce any vegetable into its three first principles. Then join them together again, being well purified, and put the same into a rich earth, and you shall have it produce a vegetable far more glorious than any of its species.

Now, how to make such an essence, look into the first book, and there you shall see the process thereof.

TO MAKE A PLANT GROW IN TWO OR THREE HOURS

Take the ashes of moss and moisten them with the juice of an old dunghill, being first pressed forth and strained. Then dry them a little, and moisten them as before. Do this four or five times. Put this mixture, being neither very dry nor very moist, into some earthen or metal vessel, and in it set the seeds of lettuce, purslain or parsley (because they will grow sooner than other plants) being first impregnated with the essence of a vegetable of its own species (the process thereof you shall find in Book I) until they begin to sprout forth. Then, I say, put them in the said earth with that end upwards which sprouts forth. Then put the vessel into a gentle heat, and when it begins to dry moisten it with some of the said juice of dung.
You may by this means have a salad grow while supper is making ready.

TO MAKE THE IDEA OF ANY PLANT APPEAR IN A GLASS AS IF THE VERY PLANT ITSELF WERE THERE

The process of this you may see in Book I and, therefore, I need not here again repeat it. Only remember that if you put the flame of a candle to the bottom of the glass where the essence is, by which it may be made hot, you will see that thin substance which is like impalpable ashes or salt send forth from the bottom of the glass the manifest form of a vegetable, vegetating and growing by little and little, and putting on so fully the form of stalks, leaves, and flowers in such perfect and natural wise in apparent show that anyone would believe verily the same to be naturally corporeal when as, in truth, it is the spiritual idea, induced with a spiritual essence which serves for no other purpose but to be matched with its fitting earth, so that it may take unto itself a more solid body. This shadowed figure, as soon as the vessel is taken from the fire, returns to its ashes again and vanishes away, becoming a chaos and confused matter.

TO MAKE FIR TREES APPEAR IN TURPENTINE

Take as much turpentine as you please and put it into a retort. Distill it by degrees. When all is distilled off, keep the retort still in a reasonable heat so that what humidity is still remaining may be evaporated and it become dry. Then take this off from the fire and hold your hand to the bottom of the retort. The turpentine that is dried (which is called colophonia) will crack asunder in several places, and in those cracks or chaps you shall see the perfect effigies of fir trees which will there continue many months.

TO MAKE HARTSHORN SEEMINGLY TO GROW IN A GLASS

Take hartshorn broken into small pieces, and put them into a glass retort to be distilled. You shall see the glass to be seemingly full of horns which will continue there so long until the volatile salt comes over.

TO MAKE GOLDEN MOUNTAINS AS IT WERE APPEAR IN A GLASS

Take of adders eggs half a pound, and put them into a glass retort. Distill them by degrees. When all is dry, you shall see the feces at the bottom turgid and puffed up and seem to be, as it were, golden mountains, being very glorious to behold.

TO MAKE THE REPRESENTATION OF THE WHOLE WORLD IN A GLASS

Take of the purest salt nitre as much as you please, and of tin half as much. Mix them together and calcine them hermetically. Then put them into a retort, to which annex a glass receiver, and lute them well together. Let there be leaves of gold put into the bottom thereof. Then put fire to the retort until vapors arise that will cleave to the gold. Augment the fire until no more fumes ascend. Then take away the receiver and close it hermetically. Make a lamp fire under it, and you will see represented in it the sun, moon, stars, fountains, flowers, trees, fruits and, indeed, even all things which is a glorious sight to behold.

TO MAKE FOUR ELEMENTS APPEAR IN A GLASS

Take of the subtle powder of jeat one ounce and a half, of the oil of tartar made per deliqulum (in which there is not one drop of water besides what the tartar itself contracted) two ounces which you must color with a light green with vardegrease, of the purest spirit of wine tinged with a light blue with indigo, two ounces of the best rectified spirit of turpentine colored with a light red with madder. Put all these into a glass and shake them together. You shall see the jeat which is heavy and black fall to the bottom and represent the earth. Next, the oil of tartar made green representing the element of water falls. Upon that swims the blue spirit of wine which will not mix with the oil of tartar, and represents the element of air, uppermost will swim the subtle red oil of turpentine which represent the element of fire.

It is strange to see how after shaking all these together they will be distinctly separated the one from the other. If it be well done, as it is easy enough to do, it is a most glorious sight.

TO MAKE A PERPETUAL MOTION IN A GLASS

Take seven ounces of quicksilver, as much tin, and grind them well together with fourteen ounces of sublimate dissolved in a cellar upon a marble the space of four days. It will become like oil of olive, which distill in sand. There will sublime a dry substance. Then put the water which distills off back upon the earth in the bottom of the still, and dissolve what you can. Filter it and distill it again. This do four or five times. Then that earth will be so subtle that, being put into a vial, the subtle atoms thereof will move up and down forever.

Note that the vial or glass must be close stopped and kept in a dry place.

TO MAKE A LUMINOUS WATER THAT SHALL GIVE LIGHT BY NIGHT

Take the tails of glowworms, put them into a glass still, and distill them in balneum. Pour the said water upon more fresh tails of glowworms.

Do this four or five times and you shall have a most luminous water by which you may see to read in the darkest night.

Some say this water may be made of the skins of herring, and for ought I know, it may be probable enough. For I have heard that a shoal of herring coming by a ship in the night have given a great light to all the ship.

It were worth the while to know the true reason why glowworms and herring and some other such like things should be luminous in the night.

TO MAKE A VAPOR IN A CHAMBER THAT HE THAT ENTERS INTO IT WITH A CANDLE SHALL THINK THE ROOM TO BE ON FIRE

Dissolve camphor in rectified aqua vitae and evaporate them in a very close chamber where no air can get in. He that first enters the chamber with a lighted candle will be much astonished, for the chamber will seem to be full of fire, very subtle, but it will be of little continuance. You must note that it is the combustible vapor, with which the chamber is filled, that takes the flame from the candle.

Diverse such like experiments as this may be done by putting such a combustible vapor into a box, or cupboard, or such like which will as soon as anyone shall open them, having a candle in his hand, take fire and burn.

TO MAKE POWDER THAT BY SPITTING UPON SHALL BE INFLAMED

Take a loadstone, powder it, and put it into a strong calcining pot. Cover it all over with a powder made of calx vive and colophonia, of each a like quantity, and also put some of this powder under it. When the pot is full, cover it and lute the closures with potters earth. Put them into a furnace and there let them boil. Then take them out and put them into another pot. Set them in the furnace again, and this do until they become a very white and dry calx. Take of this calx one part, of salt nitre very well purified four parts, and as much camphor, sulphur vivum, and the oil of turpentine and tartar. Grind all these to a subtle powder and searse them, and put them into a glass vessel. Then put as much spirit of wine well rectified as will cover them two fingers breadth. Then close them up and set the vessel in horse dung three months, and in that time they will all become a uniform paste. Evaporate all the humidity until the whole mass becomes a very dry stone. Then take it out and powder it, and keep it very dry.

If you take a little of this powder and spit upon it, or pour some water upon it, it will take fire presently, so that you may light a match or any such thing by it.

TO FORTIFY A LOADSTONE THAT IT SHALL BE ABLE TO DRAW A NAIL OUT OF A PIECE OF WOOD

Take a loadstone and heat it very hot in coals, but so that it be not fired. Then presently quench it in the oil of crocus martis, made of the best steel, so that it may imbibe as much as it can.

You shall by this means make the loadstone so very strong and powerful that you may pull out nails from a piece of wood with it, and do such wonderful things with it that the common loadstone can never do.

Now the reason of this (as Paracelsus says) is because the spirit of iron is the life of the loadstone, and this may be extracted from or increased in the loadstone.

TO MAKE QUICKSILVER MALLEABLE IN SEVEN HOURS

Take of the best lead, melt it, and pour it into a hole. When it is almost congealed, make a hole in it, and presently fill up the hole with quicksilver, and it will presently become congealed into a friable substance. Then beat it into a powder, and put it again into a hole of fresh melted lead as before. Do this three or four times. Then boil it, being all in a piece of linseed oil, the space of six hours. Then take it out and it will become malleable.

Note that after this it may, by being melted over the fire, be reduced into quicksilver again.

A thin plate of the said mercury laid upon an inveterate ulcer takes away the malignity of it in a great measure and renders it more curable than before.

A plate of said mercury laid upon tumors would be a great deal better repercussive than plates of lead which surgeons use in such cases.
The powder of the friable substance of mercury before it be boiled in the oil is very good to be strewed upon old ulcers, for it does much to correct the virulency of them.

TO REDUCE GLASS INTO ITS FIRST PRINCIPLES VIZ. SAND AND SALT

Take bits or powder of glass, as much as you please, and as much of the salt which glassmen use in the making of glasses. Melt these together in a strong fire. Then dissolve all the melted mass in warm water. Then pour off the water and you shall see no glass, but only sand in the bottom, which sand is that which was in the glass before.
This confutes the vulgar opinion, namely that the fusion of glass is the last fusion and beyond all reduction.

TO WRITE OR ENGRAVE UPON AN EGG OR PIBBLE WITH WAX OR GREASE

Make what letters or figures you please with wax or grease upon an egg or pibble. Put them into the strongest spirit of vinegar, and there let them lie two or three days. You shall see every place about the letters or figures eaten or consumed away with the said spirit. But the place where the wax or grease was is not at all touched. The reason whereof is because the spirit would not operate upon the said oleaginous matter.

TO MAKE ARTIFICIAL PEARL AS GLORIOUS AS ANY ORIENTAL

Dissolve mother of pearl in spirit of vinegar. Then precipitate it with oil of sulphur per campanum (and not with oil of tartar, for that takes away the splendor of it) which adds a luster to it. When it is thus precipitated, dry it, and mix it with white of eggs, and of this mass you may make pearls of what bigness or fashion you please. Before they be dried, you may make holes through them. When they be dried they will not at all, or very hardly, be discerned from true and natural pearls.

TO MAKE A MINERAL PERFUME

Dissolve antimony or sulphur in the liquor or oil of flints or pebbles, or crystals, or sand. Coagulate the solution into a red mass, pour thereon the spirit of urine, and digest them until the spirit be tinged. Then pour it off and pour more on until all the tincture be extracted. Put all the tinctures together and evaporate the spirit of unine in balneum. There will remain a blood red liquor at the bottom, upon which pour spirit of wine, and you shall extract a purer tincture which smells like garlic. Digest it three or four weeks, and it will smell like balm. Digest it longer and it will smell like musk or ambergris.

Besides the smell that it has, it is an excellent sudorific, and cures all diseases that require sweat: as the plague, putrid fevers, lues venerea, and such like as these.

THE OIL OR LIQUOR OF SAND, FLINTS, PEBBLES, OR CRYSTALS FOR THE AFORESAID PREPARATION IS MADE THUS

Take of the best salt of tartar, being very well purified by two or three dissolutions and coagulations, and powdered in a hot mortar, one part. Of flints, pebbles, or crystals, being powdered, or small sand well washed, the fourth part. Mingle them well together. Put as much of this composition as will fill an eggshell into a crucible. Set in the earthen furnace (described in Book III) and made red hot. Presently there will come over a thick and white spirit. This do until you have enough. Then take out of the crucible while it is glowing hot, and that which is in it is like transparent glass, which keep from the air.

The spirit may be rectified by sand in a glass retort.

This spirit is of excellent use in the gout, stone, ptisick, and indeed in all obstructions. It provokes sweat, urine, and cleanses the stomach and, by consequence, is effectual in most diseases.

It being applied externally clears the skin and makes it look very fair. Take that which remains at the bottom in the crucible and beat it to powder, and lay it in a moist place so that it dissolves into a thick fat oil. And this is that which is called the oil of sand, of flints, pebbles, or crystals.

This oil is of wonderful use in medicine, as also in the preparation of all sorts of minerals.

This oil, being taken inwardly in some appropriate liquor, dissolves tartarous coagulations in the body, and so opens all obstructions. It precipitates metals and makes the calx thereof more weighty than oil of tartar does.

It is of a golden nature. It extracts colors from all metals, is fixed in all fires, makes fine crystals and borax, and matures imperfect metals into gold.

If you put it into water, there will precipitate a most fine white earth, of which you may make as clear vessels as are china dishes. Note that all sand, flints, and pebbles, even the whitest, have in them a golden sulphur or tincture, and if a prepared lead be for a time digested in this oil it will seem, as it were, gilded because of the gold that will hang upon it which may be washed away in water. Gold also is found in sand and flints, etc., and if you put gold into this oil it will become more ponderous thereby.

TO MAKE STEEL GROW IN A GLASS LIKE A TREE

Dissolve steel in a rectified spirit of salt, so shall you have a green and sweet solution which smells like brimstone. Filter it and abstract all the moisture in sand with a gentle heat. There will distill over a liquor as sweet as rain water. Steel, by reason of its dryness, detains the corrosiveness of the spirit of salt which remains in the bottom like a blood red mass which is as hot on the tongue as fire. Dissolve this red mass in oil of flints or of sand, and you shall see it grow up in two or three hours like a tree with stem and branches. Prove this tree at the test, and it shall yield good gold which this tree has drawn from the aforesaid oil of sand or flints which has a golden sulphur in it.

TO MELT A METAL IN ONE'S HAND WITHOUT BURNING OF THE HAND

Take a little calcining pot in your hand. Make in it a lane or course of the powder of any metal. Then upon it lay a lane of sulphur, saltpeter, and saw dust, of each a like quantity, mixed together. Put a coal of fire to it, and forthwith the metal will be melted into a mass.

AN OBSERVATION UPON THE BEAMS OF THE SUN AND HEAT OF THE FIRE HOW THEY ADD WEIGHT TO MINERAL & METAL BODIES

Take of any mineral liquor and set it in an open vessel in the sun for a good space, and it will be augmented in quantity and weight. But some will say that this proceeds from the air, to the which I answer and demand whether the air had not this impregnation from the sun, and what the air has in itself that proceeds not from the sun and stars. Put this liquor in a cold cellar or in a moist air, and you shall find that it increases not in weight, as it does in the sun or in the fire (which has in this respect some analogy with the sun). I do not say but haply it might attract some little moisture which is soon exhaled by any small heat.

Dissolve any sulphurous and imperfect metal, as iron, copper, or zinc, in aqua fortis or any other acid spirit. Then abstract the spirit from it. Make it glowing hot, yet not too hot, so that the spirit may only vapor away. Then weigh this metal calx and set it in a crucible over the fire. But melt it not, only let it darkly glow, let it stand so three or four weeks, and then take it off and weigh it again. You shall find it heavier than before.

Set any sulphurous metal, as iron or copper, with sixteen or eighteen parts of lead on a test made with ashes of wood or bones in a probatory furnace. First weigh the test copper and lead before you put them into the furnace. Let the iron or copper fly away with the lead, yet not with toe strong a heat. Then take the test out and weigh it, and you shall find it (though the metals be gone) when it is cold to be heavier than it was when it was put into the furnace with the metals. The question is now whence this heaviness of all the aforesaid minerals and metals proceeded, if that the heat of the sun and fire through the help of the minerals and metals be not fixed into a palpable mineral and metal body?

Set a test with lead or copper in the sun. With a concave glass unite the beams of the sun, and let them fall on the center of the metal. Hold the concave glass in your hand, and let your test never be cold. This will be as well done in the sun as in the fire. But this concave must be two feet in diameter, and not too hollow or deep, but about the eighteenth or twentieth part of the circle, so that it may the better cast its beams forth. It must be very well polished.

Calcine antimony with a burning glass and you shall see it smoke and fume and be made drier than before, yet weigh it and it will be heavier than before.

I shall take in, for the confirmation of all this, a relation of Sir Kenelme Digby concerning the precipitating of the sun beams. I remember (says he) a rare experiment that a nobleman of much sincerity and a singular friend of mine told me he had seen which was, that by means of glasses made in a very particular manner and artificially placed one by another, he had seen the sun beams gathered together and precipitated down to a brownish or purplish red powder. There (says he) could be no fallacy in this operation. For nothing whatsoever was in the glass when they were placed and disposed for this intent. And it must be in the hot time of the year, else the effect would not follow. Of this magistery he could gather some days nearly two ounces, and it was a strong volatile virtue, and would impress its spiritual quality into gold itself (the heaviest and most fixed body we converse withal!) in a very short time.

I leave it now to the reader to judge whether the beams of the sun and and the heat of the fire add weight to minerals and metals.

TO EXTRACT A WHITE MILKY SUBSTANCE FROM THE RAYS OF THE MOON

Take a concave glass and hold it against the moon when she is at the full in a clear evening. Let the rays thereof being united fall upon a sponge, and the sponge will be full of a cold milky substance which you may press out with your hand and gather more. De-La-Brosse is of the opinion that this substance is of the substance of the moon, but I cannot assent to him in that. Only this I say, if this experiment were well prosecuted, it might produce, for ought I know, such a discovery which might be the key to no small secrets.

TO CONDENSE THE AIR IN THE HEAT OF SUMMER AND IN THE HEAT OF THE DAY INTO WATER

Fill an earthen vessel unglazed, made pointed downward, and fill it with snow water (which must be kept all the year) in which is dissolved as much nitre as the water would dissolve. Let the vessel be close stopped. Hold this vessel against the sun and the air will be so condensed by the coldness of the vessel that if will drop down by the sides thereof.

HOW TWO SORTS OF VOLATILE SALTS WILL BE FIXED BY JOINING THEM TOGETHER

Take a strong lixivium made of unslaked lime, and evaporate it. Whereas you would expect to find a salt at the bottom, there is none, for all the salt in the lixivium is vapored away, and the more the liquor is evaporated the weaker the lixivium becomes, which is contrary to other lixiviums. Also, if you take the spirit of vinegar and evaporate it, you shall find no salt at the bottom. Now, if you take the clear lixivium of lime and spirit of vinegar, of each a like quantity, and mix them together and evaporate the humidity thereof, you shall find a good quantity of salt at the bottom which tastes partly hot and partly acid. This salt, being set in a cold cellar on a marble stone and dissolved into an oil, is as good as any lac virginis to clear and smooth the face and dry up any hot pustules in the skin, as also against the itch and old ulcers to dry them up.

TO MAKE AN UNGUENT THAT A FEW GRAINS THEREOF BEING APPLIED OUTWARDLY WILL CAUSE VOMITING OR LOOSNESS AS YOU PLEASE

Take lapis infernalis and mix therewith of distilled oil of tobacco as much as will make an ointment. Keep it in a dry place.

If you would provoke vomiting, anoint the pit of the stomach with five or six grains thereof, and the party will presently vomit, and as much as with taking of vomit.

If you would provoke to loosness, anoint about the navel therewith, and the patient will presently fall into a loosness.

Note that you must give the patient some warm suppings all the time this medicine is working.

Note also, and that especially, that you let not the ointment lie so long as to cauterize the part to which it is applied.

HOW TO MAKE A MEDICINE THAT HALF A GRAIN THEREOF BEING TAKEN EVERY MORNING WILL KEEP THE BODY SOLUBLE

Take of the distilled oil of tobacco, of which let the essential salt of tobacco imbibe as much as it can. Then with this composition make some lozenges by adding such things as are fitting for such a form of medicine. Note that you put but such a quantity of this oily salt as half a grain only may be in one lozenge.

One of these lozenges being taken every morning or every other morning keeps the body soluble, and is good for them as are apt to be very costive in their bodies.

Note that you may put some aromatical ingredient into the lozenges that may qualify the offensive odor of the oil, if there shall be any.

TO MAKE A CORDIAL STOMACHICAL AND PURGATIVE TINCTURE

Make a tincture of hierapera with spirit of wine well rectified and aromatized with cinnamon or cloves.

Two or three spoonfuls of this tincture being taken in a morning twice in a week wonderfully helps those that have weak and foul stomachs. It opens obstructions and purges viscosities of the stomach and bowels, cures all inveterate headaches, kills worms and, indeed, leaves no impurities in the body, and is very cordial. For it exceedingly helps them that are troubled with faintings. There is nothing offensive in this medicine but the bitterness thereof which the other extraordinary virtues will more than balance.

ANOTHER

Dissolve scammony in spirit of wine. Evaporate the one moiety. Then precipitate it by putting rose water to it, and it will become most white, for the black and fetid matter will lie on the top of the precipitated matter which you must wash away with rose water. Then take that white gum, being very well washed, and dry it. (If you please, you may powder it and so use it. For indeed it has neither smell nor taste, and purges without any offence. It may be given to children, or to any that distaste physic, in their milk or broth without any discerning of it and, indeed, it does purge without any manner of grippings. I was wont to make it up into pills with oil of cinnamon or cloves which gave it a gallant smell, and of which I gave a scruple which wrought moderately and without any manner of grippings). Then dissolve it again in spirit of wine, being aromatized with what spices you please, and this keep. This tincture is so pleasant, so gentle, so noble a purgative that there is scarce the like in the world, for it purges without any offence, is taken without any nauseating, and purges all manner of humors, especially cholera and melancholy, and is very cordial.

It may be given to those that abhor any medicine, as to children or those that are of a nauseous stomach.

The dose is from half a spoonful to two or three.

Note it must be taken of itself, for if it be put into any other liquor the scammony will precipitate and fall to the bottom.

After this manner, you may prepare jollap by extracting the gum therefrom and then dissolving it in spirit of wine.

By this means jollap would not be so offensive to the stomach, as usually it is, for it is the gum that is purgative and the earthliness that is so nauseous.

Jollap being thus prepared is a most excellent medicine against all hydropic diseases, for it purges water away without any nausea or griping at all.

TO REDUCE DISTILLED TURPENTINE INTO ITS BODY AGAIN

Take of oil of turpentine and the colophonia thereof (which is that substance which remains in the bottom after distillation) which you must beat to powder. Mix these together and digest them, and you shall have a turpentine of the same consistency as before, but of a fiery subtle nature.

Pills made of this turpentine are of excellent use in obstructions of the breast, kidneys, and the like.

TO MAKE THE DISTILLED OIL OUT OF ANY HERB, SEED, OR FLOWER IN AN INSTANT WITHOUT ANY FURNACE

You must have a long pipe made of tin which must have a bowl in the middle with a hole in it as big as you can put your finger into it, by which you must put your matter that you would have the oil of. Set this matter on fire with a candle or coal of fire. Then put one end of the pipe into a basin of fair water and blow at the other end, and the smoke will come into the water, and there will an oil swim upon the water which you may separate with a tunnel.

TO MAKE WATER AND THE TINCTURE OF ANY VEGETABLE AT THE SAME TIME WHICH IS AN EXCELLENT WAY TO DRAW OUT THE VIRTUE THEREOF

This must be performed by these following vessels.

A. Signifies the furnace itself.

B. The retort which stands in water or sand, wherein the matter to be distilled is put, instead, whereof if you please you may put a gourd glass with a head to it.

C. The pipe.

D. Another vessel where is more fresh matter, out of which the tincture is to be drawn, and which stands upon ashes with a fire under it.

E. The furnace with a pan of ashes.

F The receiver.

G. The hole of the furnace to put in coals to heat the second matter.

A WAY TO SEPARATE FRESH WATER FROM SALT WITHOUT A FURNACE OR MUCH TROUBLE

Take a cauldron with a great and high cover having a beak or nose, set it upon a trivet, and under it put a fire. Let this be filled with salt water, and there will presently distill off a good quantity of fresh water into a receiver which must be joined to the nose of the aforesaid cover.

This is of good use for seamen that want fresh water, for by this means they may distill a good quantity in 24 hours, especially if they have any considerable number of the aforesaid vessels, a figure whereof is this which follows.

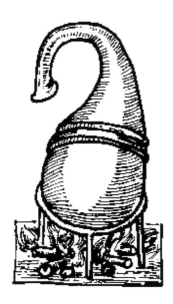

A WAY TO PURGE AND PURIFY TROUBLED AND MUDDY WATERS

Fill a great pot with puddled water, and put a soft and gentle fire under it. Lay some bricks across on the pot brims, and upon the sticks lay clean wool or a sponge well washed. Now the wool drinks up the vapors that ascend which you then must wring out and lay on the wool again. This you may do until you have as much clean water as you desire. The manner of this distillation is described thus.

A. Signifies the pot.
B. The fire.
C. The sticks.
D. The wool.
This is of use for them that can come at no other waters but what are troubled, as it falls out many times in some places.

ANY THICK ANOTHER WAY TO PURIFY MUDDY, OR FECULENT LIQUOR

This is performed by shreds of any white woolen cloth in vessels as you can see hereafter expressed.

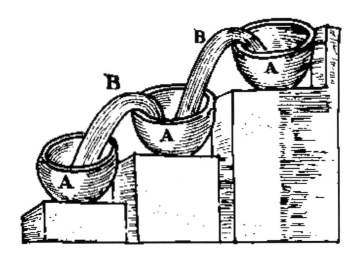

A. Signifies the vessels.
B. The shreds.

Note that the shreds must be first wet in fair water, and the feculent matter be put into the uppermost vessel.

Note also, whereas here be two receivers, that in many cases one may be sufficient.

This way serves for the purifying of decoctions, juices, or diesolutions of salts from their feculency, for that which is distilled by the shreds is as clear as crystal, when what remains is very feculent.

TO KEEP FIRE IN A GLASS THAT WHILE THE GLASS IS SHUT WILL NOT BURN BUT AS SOON AS IT IS OPENED WILL BE INFLAMED

First extract the burning spirit of the salt of tin in a glass retort well coated. When the retort is cold, take it out and break it, and as soon as the matter in it which remains in the bottom thereof after distillation comes into the air, it will presently be inflamed. Put this matter into a glass vial, and keep it close stopped.

This fire will keep many thousand years and not burn unless the glass be opened. But at what time soever that it is opened, it will burn.

It is conceived that such a kind of fire as this was found in vaults when they were opened which many conceived to be a perpetual burning lamp, when as indeed it was inflamed at the opening the vault and the letting in air thereby which before it lacked and, therefore, could not burn. For it is to be conceived that there is no fire burns longer than its matter endures, and there is no combustible matter can endure forever. There may be many uses of such a fire as this, for any man may carry it about with him and let it burn on a sudden when he has any occasion for fire.

A lamp furnace is made thus.

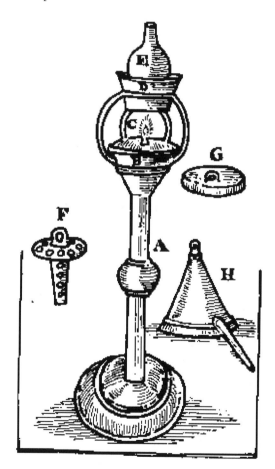

A. Signifies the candlestick which must be hollow and full of water.

B. The top of the candlestick which must be wide to contain good store of water for to fill up the candlestick as the candle rises up.

C. The candle which must be as long as the candlestick.

D. The vessel that contains either water, sand, or ashes for any vessel to be set into, also to contain any matter itself that is to be distilled or digested.

E. A glass vessel standing in digestion.

F. A narrow-mouthed stopple to be put into the candlestick to keep the candle upright, and that must be made of tin with holes in it.

G. The cover for the vessel D which is to be put upon it when anything is decocted or kept warm in it.

H. A still head to put upon the vessel D when you would distill anything in it.

Note that if you make all these vessels large you may do many considerable things without much labor or trouble.

In the vessel D, if it be large, you may stew meat which, if you put in at night and cover it close, you may have it ready for your breakfast in the morning and so, according to the time you put it in, you may have it for dinner or supper. Also, you may keep anything warm in the night and at all times, diverse such uses as these it may be used for.

Note that the candle will still rise up until it be quite burned out, and an ordinary candle will last twice as long this way as it will out of the water.

If you would have one candle last a long time, as twelve or twenty hours, you must either make your candlestick very long that it may contain a long candle, or make your candle big and the wick small, or make your candle of such matter as will not presently be consumed. Note also that if you would have a great heat, your candle must be great, and also the wick thereof great, but if gentle, let your candle be s mall.

ANOTHER LAMP FURNACE

There is another sort of lamp furnace with three candles after this manner.

The use of this is when you would have a constant fire that should give a stronger heat than one candle in the former furnace. And the truth is that if your candles be big (as you may make them as big as you will) you may have as strong a heat this way as by ashes in an ordinary furnace.

TO MAKE A CANDLE THAT SHALL LAST LONG

Take unslaked lime, powder it and mix it with your tallow, and so make you candle of that. Or else, you may make candles of castile soap which will serve for such uses as these, viz., to burn in such a lamp furnace. Note that it is the salt that is in the lime and soap that preserves the the tallow from burnig out so fast as otherwise it would.

TO MAKE A LASTING AND DURABLE OIL

Take unslaked lime, bay salt, oil of olive, of each a like quantity, and mix them well together and distill them in sand. Cohobate the oil upon the same quantity of fresh lime and salt, and this do four or five times.

By this means will the oil be clear and impregnated with what salt was volatile in the lime and salt.

Now that saline impregnation is that which gives a durableness to the oil.

Note that this oil while it is distilling is of a most fragrant smell. I have some of it which I distilled seven times and it is as pure, subtle, and odoriferous as many common distilled oils and vegetables.

This oil, besides the durability of it, is also good against any inveterate ache in the limbs.

A lamp made with this oil will continue burning six times as long as a lamp made of other oil. Also, it burns very sweet.

There must be a great deal of care used in making of it, or else you will quickly break your glasses. Also, you must take very strong lime, such as the dyers use, and call cauke.

PHILOSOPHICAL BELLOWS

There be here set down three figures of these kinds of instruments which belong to several uses.

A. Signifies that which blows a fire for the melting of any metal or such like operation, and it blows most forcibly with a terrible noise.

B. That which blows a candle to make the flame thereof very strong for the melting of glasses and nipping them up.

C. That which anyone may hold in their hand to blow up the fire strongly upon any occasion.

Now the manner of the using of them is this. You must first heat them very hot. Then put the noses thereof (which must have a very small hole in them, no bigger than that a pin's head may go in) into a vessel of cold water. They will presently suck in the water, of which then being full, turn the noses thereof towards the candle or fire which you would have blown.

As for the figure C, it must have a mouth drawn up around and hanging out an inch from the face, which mouth (the whole compass of the face being heated first) you must dip in cold water, and it will suck in water as the noses of the former did. This then you must hold close to the fire that it may be heated, and it will blow exceedingly, as otherwise it will not, viz., if it be cold.

If you put sweet water into such a vessel, you may perfume a chamber exceedingly, for a little quantity thereof will be a long time breathing forth.

Note that these kinds of vessels must be made of copper and be exceedingly well closed so that they may have no vent but by their noses.

AN EXCELLENT INVENTION TO MAKE A FIRE

Take three parts of the best Newcastle coals beaten small and one part of loam. Mix these well together into a mass with water. Make thereof balls which you must dry very well.

This fire is durable, sweet, not offensive by reason of the smoke or cinder as other coal fires are. It is beautiful in shape and is not so costly as other fires. It burns as well in a chamber even as charcoal.

This fire may either serve for such distillations as require a strong and lasting heat or for ordinary uses either in the kitchen or chambers.

A NEW INVENTION FOR BATHS

Seeing that by bathing and sweating most diseases are cured, especially such as proceed from wind, hot and distempered humors or cold and congealed humors, because all these are rarified and evaporated by transpiration in sweating or bathing, I thought it a thing much conducing to man's health to set down such a way of bathing and sweating that might be very effectual and appropriated to any particular disease or distemper.

I shall therefore here commend to you a way of bathing by distillation, the manner of which you may see by these ensuing vessels.

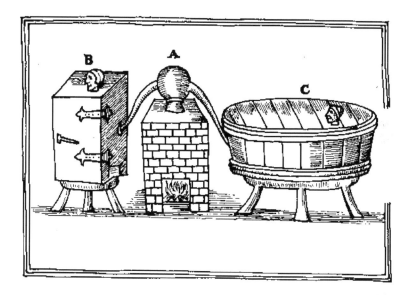

A. Signifies a hot still with two pipes going into two wooden vessels. In this still you may put either herbs, spices, with water or with spirits, and distill them, by which means they that are in the vessels will presently be forced into a sweat by virtue of the subtlety of the vapors. And this indeed is as good and effectual a way for sweating as any can be invented. You may by this means appropriate your ingredients to the nature of the diseases.

B. A vessel wherein a man sits in the bath. Now this vessel has in it a door for the easier going into it, which fashion is far better and more convenient, than to be open only at the top.

C. A long vessel where a man that is weak, and not able to sit up, lies and is bathed.

Now you must note that these vapors must not be hotter than the patient can bear. Also, if the vapor comes forth too hot upon the body of the patient, he may by putting a pipe upon the end of the pipe that comes into the vessel, divert the hot vapor from his body, and so it will not offend him that way.

Note that the patient, as soon as he begins to be faint, must come forth or else he will suffer more prejudice than good by his bathing. Also, to prevent him from fainting let him take some cordial or cold beer which will revive him and make him endure his bathing longer, as also make him sweat the more.

As soon as the patient comes forth, let him go into a warm bed and sweat as he is able to bear it, and take some posses drink or broth or such like warm suppings, as also some good cordial if he be very faint. The patient may, according to his strength and his disease, bathe more seldom or oftener.

AN ARTIFICIAL BATH MADE FROM THE SAME PRINCIPLES AS THE NATURAL BATH IS

Before I set down the process of making an artificial hot bath, I shall premise something concerning the true nature and origin of a hot bath. Now the clearest and best account that I ever heard or read of the cause of the heat in baths is that which is given by Monsieur de Rochas, and that in a demonstrative way. His words are these:

"As I was", says he, "with some of my companions wandering in Savoy, I found in the valley of Lucerne between the Alps a hot spring. I began to consider the cause of this heat, and whereas the vulgar opinion is that the heat of fountains is from mountains fired within, I saw reason to think the contrary because I saw snow upon a mountain from whence this hot spring came, unmelted, which could not have been possible, but would have been dissolved by the hot fumes of the mountains had they been fired. Whereupon, being unsatisfied, I with my companions and other laborers (whom I could hardly persuade to undertake such a business by reason they were afraid that fire would thereupon break forth out of the ground and consume us) got tools and set upon digging to find out the true cause of the heat of this fountain. After we had dug fifteen days (having before perceived the water to be hotter and hotter by degrees as we came nearer to the source) we came to the original of the heat where was a great ebullition. In three hours more we dug beyond this place of ebullition and perceived the water to be cold, yet in the same continued stream with the other that was hot. Upon this I began to wonder much at the reason of these things. Then I carried to by lodging some of this hot water (which was both saltish and acid) and evaporated it. Of forty ounces I yet further purified and extracted thence three drams of pure nitrous hermetic salt, the other two ounces being a slimy sulphurous substance. Yet with this I was not satisfied, but with my laborers went again to the place and dug twelve days more. Then we came to a water which was insipid as ordinary fountain water, yet still in a continued stream with the saltish and hot water. At this I wondered much, whereupon I dug up some of the earth where the cold and saltish stream ran and carried it home with me, and out of a hundred weight thereof I extracted a good quantity of nitrous salt which was almost fluxile.

'When I extracted as much as I could, I laid the earth aside, and in 24 hours it was all covered over with salt which I extracted, and out of a hundred weight of this earth, which I call virgin earth, I had four pounds of this kind of salt which it contracted in the aforesaid 24 hours, and so it would do constantly. Now this satisfied me concerning one doubt. For before I was unsatisfied how there could be a constant supply of that salt which made the water saltish, seeing there was but a little distance between the insipid water and the hot water, and the constant stream of water washed away the salt which was in that little space. For I perceived that this kind of earth attracts this universal salt of the world partly from the air in the cavities of the earth and partly from the vapors that constantly pass through the earth. After this I took some of that earth where the ebullition was and carried it home and proved it, and I perceived it to be a sulphur mine, into which the former acid saltish water penetrating caused an ebullition, as do salt of tartar and spirit of vitriol being mixed together, and also water poured on unslaked lime. After this I began to question how it was that this sulphur mine was not consumed, seeing so much matter pass from it daily. But when I began to understand how all things in the earth did assimilate to themselves whatsoever was of any kind of affinity to them, as as mines convert the tools of miners into their own substance in a little time, and such like experiments of that nature, I was satisfied. And after all this I understood how this universal salt of the world was to be had, and I could at any time mix it with water, and pour that water upon sulphur, and so make an artificial hot bath as good as any natural bath whatsoever. Note that no salt in the world but this nitrous salt will do it, as I often tried. And this salt is to be found in all hot baths, and to be prepared artificially. " Thus far Monsieur de Rochas.

Something like unto this Helmont seems to hold forth, saying that there is a Primum Ens Salium or Femina Salium which are all seated in waters and vapors and give them an acidity, but as yet have no saline taste until they meet with such principles and be received into certain matrixes in the earth which may make them put forth this potential saltiness into act. According to this diversity of places this water or vapor, being impregnated with those seeds of salt, goes through arise the diversity of salts, as alum, sea salt, nitre, etc. Then upon this account the earth, through which the cold, acid, saltish water abovesaid run through, did specificate that potential salt which was both in the water and vapors into a nitrous salt (by which means was that kind of salt in that place). But whether this Prium Ens Salium by so unspecificated or Quid Hermaphroditicum as he asserts, or no, it matters not much to my purpose. It suffices if that earth, through which that acid nitrous water runs, attracts and multiplies an acid nitrous salt with which the water, being impregnated and running through a sulphurous mine, causes an ebullition. All this being premised, I shall now endeavor to illustrate how nature may in this be imitated, as that an artificial hot bath may be made by such like principles, as the natural hot bath consists of, being artificially prepared.

Now these principles are the sulphur mine and the acid nitrous salt. The former requires no further preparation (as says Monsieur de Rochas) if it be pure. The latter is to be prepared two manner of ways. Either it is to be extracted, as says the foresaid author, out of the waters of the bath by evaporating them away, or by condensing the nitrous air (for indeed as many judicious philosophers are of opinion, the air is wholly nitrous as it appears by the condensation of it in cold places into nitre) which his virgin earth did do into a salt which was acid and almost fluxile. Now when I say that the nitrous salt is to be thus prepared, I do not say that this is the full preparation thereof, for indeed it is yet further to be prepared, and that is by giving it a greater acidity.

I question much whether or no the salt, being prepared after the aforesaid ways, does retain that acidity which is required for that ebullition I spoke of, and which the nitrous water had before it came to the mine of sulphur. For indeed, the aforesaid author when he affirmed that he could at any time make an artificial hot bath, did not say he used the salt prepared only after the two former ways, viz., by extracting it out of the waters of the bath and making it with his virgin earth which did attract and condense the nitrousness of the air, but withall by making it so acid that it might cause an ebullition when it came to be joined with a sulphur mine.

Now then, how to give this nitre a sufficient acidity is the great question. For the better effecting of this we must consider whence that nitrous water (above mentioned) in the earth had the greatest part of its acidity.

As to that, it must be remembered that the virgin earth through which the acid nitrous water did run, did condense the nitrous air or vapors into a nitrous salt and, withal!, it is to be considered that before this nitrous air or vapor, before it is condensed, even when it is near unto condensation is acid, and part of it before condensation is mixed with the water, and so renders it acid. Now that waters have a great part of their acidity from the acid vapors of acid minerals both Henricus ab Heers and Jordan upon mineral waters affirm. That salts unbodied are far more acid than when they have assumed a body is clearly manifest in this, viz., that spirits of salts which I call salts unbodied, because they have lost their body, are become very acid because unbodied. If so in spirits that have lost their bodies, why not after some proportion in those that have not yet assumed a body, as vapors of nitre, or nitrous air being near to congelation, and bodying, and impregnant with spirits of nitre.

Now, I say that nitrous vapors or nitrous air, being a salt unbodied, are not so acid as spirits of nitre, because they are more phlegmatic and crude, which phlegm they lose by being congealed into a salt. Yet for all this, they are far more acid than the body of salt, and this is that which Helmont understands when he says that the esurine salt, being incorporified, is far more active in giving taste and odor than when it has received its body by becoming a specificated salt. Furthermore, how nitre shall become sufficiently acid for the aforesaid operation is the great matter to be enquired into. We must therefore consider which way we may unbody nitre (seeing it is scarce possible to get it before it has received its body). That is done two ways, either by forcing of it into a most sharp spirit, which is too acid for our intention, or by digesting the whole substance of nitre into a liquor moderately acid, which indeed serves for our purpose, and the process is this.

Take the purest nitre you can get. Dissolve it in rainwater, so as that the water imbibes as much of it as it can. Then put this nitrous water into a common earthen vessel unglazed which you must set in a cellar. You shall see this vessel in a short time to be white all over on the outside as with a hoarfrost. This whiteness is partly the flowers of the nitre, being the purest part thereof, penetrating the vessel and partly the nitrous air condensed into nitre by the coldness of the vessel, as also assimilated to the nitre that penetrated the vessel. I said by the coldness of the vessel, because such is the coldness of an earthen vessel wherein is nitre, dissolved in water, that it will being set in snow by the fireside be freezed.

This nitre you must strike off with a feather and when you have a sufficient quantity thereof, as three or four pounds, put this or the nitrous salt extracted from both waters into a bolt head of glass (a pound in each bolt head) that two parts of three be empty. Nip it up, set it in ashes, and give it a reasonable strong fire, viz., that the upper part of the bowl of the bolt head be as hot as that you can, but well suffer your hand upon it, and you shall see that the nitre will be dissolved every day a little, and in two or three months time be wholly dissolved and become acid, but not so acid as the spirit thereof. Then put it into a glass gourd with a head and distill it off. In the bottom you shall find an acid nitrous salt almost fluxile, and not unlike that salt which Monsieur de Rochas found in the evaporating of his water. Then pour the distilled nitre water upon the said salt, and then it is for your use.

The use of these principles or ingredients is this, viz., to make fountain water sufficiently acid with this nitrous liquor. Then pour it upon a sufficient quantity of the best sulphur mine or sulphur vivum in a large wooden vessel where the patient is to be bathed. You will see the water presently heated so hot as the patient is able to bear.
The inward use of these bathwaters is by reason of the nitre in them, to dissolve gross humors, open obstructions, cleanse the kidneys and bladder and, by reason of the sulphur, to dry, mollify, discuss, and

glutinate, and to help all uterine effects proceeding from cold and windy humors.

Note that they must be drunk warm and in a good quantity, or else they will do more hurt than good.

The outward use of this is for such ill effects as are in the habit of of the body and out of the veins, as of palsies, contractions, rheums, cold humors, effects of the skin and aches, for they resolve, discuss, cleanse, mollify, etc.

Now for the manner of bathing I shall not prescribe anything, but leave this to the discretion of the physician who is to give orders and directions for all the circumstances about it. For indeed everyone is not to bathe when and how he pleases, but must apply himself to an able physician and submit himself to his judgment and experience, or else may receive either prejudice or no benefit thereby.

AN ARTIFICIAL TUNBRIDGE AND EPSOM WATER

It is granted by all that tunbridge water proceeds from an iron mine, but how it contracts that acidity and that ironish and vitriolated taste and odor, seeing upon evaporation thereof, there remains little or no vitriol or salt of iron at the bottom, is the great question. Now for the solution of this, we must consider how many ways a subterranean mineral or metal may communicate its acidity to waters and that, says Henricus ab Heers, upon spew waters, it does three ways: one, when the water passing through the mines carries along with it some of the dissoluble parts of the mine, to which is consonant the saying of Aristotle that such are waters, as is the nature of those mines through which they pass, as also of Galen when he says that pure water passing through mineral mines carry with them some of the substance of the mines. The second way is when the vapors arising from fermented minerals and metals are mixed with waters. Now that vapors retain the odor and taste of those things from whence they are raised, Aristotle in his fourth book, Sublimium, affirms, and also Helmont when he says that some parts of the iron mines, being by fermentation turned into a vapor, retain the odor and taste of the mine by virtue of the acid esurine salt and are not presently reduced into a body, and also artificial vapors of the iron mines have more virtue, and active (I mean those parts that are raised by a strong fire in a furnace from the mine of iron)than iron itself when it is melted. The third way is when a great quantity of vapors arising from the aforesaid fermented mines is elevated and by the coldness of the ambient earth is turned into an acid water which, as it passes through the earth, meets with some springs of water and, mixing with them, gives them a pleasant acidity. And this is the best of all acid waters, being clear and very pure.

This being premised, I shall now proceed to the process of making artificial waters like to those of Tunbridge and Epsom.

To make tunbridge water, take of the mine or ore of iron. Beat it very small and put it into the furnace expressed on page 90 and there will come forth an acid spirit and flowers which you must mix together until the acid spirit extracts the salt out of the flowers. Then decant off the clear liquor which will have a strong taste and smell of iron.
A few drops of this liquor put into a glassful of fountain water gives it the odor and taste of tunbridge water and communicates the same operations to it.

It opens all obstructions, purges by urine, cleanses the kidneys and bladder, helps the pissing of blood, the stopping of the urine and difficulty of making water. It allays all sharp humors, cures inward ulcers and impostumes, cleanses and strengthens the stomach and liver, etc.

Note that fountain water being made moderately acid with this acid ironish liquor may be taken from a pint to six pints but, by degrees and after the taking of it, moderate exercise is to be used, and fasting to be observed until all the water be gone out of the body which will be in seven or eight hours.

Epsom water is made artificially thus. Take of the mine of alum or alum stones. Powder it very small and distill it in the furnace expressed on page 90 end there will distill over a certain acid aluminish water which must be mixed with a double quantity of nitre water (the preparation whereof is set down in the process of making the artificial hot bath). Now you must know that Epsom water has a certain kind of acid taste which is partly aluminous and partly nitrous which proceeds from nitrous air and vapors arising from the fermentation of aluminous mines, being first mixed together and then mixed with the fountains passing through the earth.

If you put a few drops of this liquor into a glassful of fountain water it will give it the odor and taste of Epsom water, that you shall scarce discern them asunder either by that odor or operation.

This water is purgative and, indeed, purges especially all sharp burning humors, cools an inflamed, and opens an obstructed body, cleanses the kidneys and bladder, cures inward ulcers and impostumes, and is a very good preservative against the consumption, etc.

Fountain water made acid with this liquor may be taken from a pint to six or eight, but by degrees, and after it moderate exercise must be used, and fasting until the water be out of the body. Only some thin warm suppings may be taken to help the working thereof. Some take this water warm.

TO MAKE ARTIFICIA L PRECIOUS STONES OF ALL SORTS OF COLORS

Take crystalline white pebble stones that are very white throughout and have no mixture of any other color which you shall find in fountains and on the sands of the sea. Put them into a crucible and make them glowing hot (covering the crucible). Then cast them into cold water, by which means they will crack and be easily reduced into a powder. Take the powder thereof and put the like quantity of pure salt of tartar thereto, which salt must not be made in any metalling, but glass vessels, so that it may have no mixture of any other colon To this mixture you may add what color you please which must be of a mineral or a metalline nature. Then put them into a very strong crucible which must be but half full and then covered, and there melt them in a strong fire until they become like glass. Note that when this mixture is in melting you must put an iron rod into it and take up some of it, and if there appears no corns of gravel in it, it is enough. If otherwise, you must melt it longer. The especial minerals and metals that give colons are these, viz., copper, iron, silver, gold, wismut, magnesia, and granite. Common copper makes a sea green; copper made out of iron, a grass green; granite, a smaragdine green; iron, yellow or a hyacinth color; silver, white yellow, green, and granite color; gold, a fine sky color; wismut common blue; magnesia, an amethyst colon And if you will mix two or three of these together, they will give other colors. For copper and silver mixed together give an amethyst color; copper and iron, a pale green; wismut and magnesia, a purple color; silver and magnesia, diverse colors like as an opal. If you would have this mass not to be transparent, but opaque, you may add the calx of tin to it when it is in melting. As if you would make lapis lazuli, then to your mixture colored with wismut add the calx of tin, and this mixture when it is almost ready to congeal cast into a mold where some powder of gold has been scattered and, by this means, it will become full of golden veins very like true lapis lazuli which is very pleasant to behold. You may by these foresaid preparations cast what forms or figures you please, of what color you please.

The metals and minerals for the making of colors ought to be thus prepared as follows.

Plates of copper must be made red hot and then quenched in cold water, of which then take five or six grains, and mix them with an ounce of the aforesaid mixture, and melt them all together and they will color it sea green.

Iron must be made into a crocus in a reverberatory fire, and then eight or ten grains thereof will tinge the mixture into a yellow or hyacinth colon

Silver is to be dissolved in aqua fortis and precipitated with oil of flints, then dulcified with water, and afterward dried. Of this five or six grains give a mingled colon

Gold must be dissolved in aqua regis, precipitated with the liquor of flints, and then sweetened and dried. Five or six grains thereof give the finest sapphire color to an ounce of the mixture.

If gold be melted with regulus martis nitrosus, five or six grains thereof give to an ounce of this mass a most incomparable rubine colon Magnesia may be powdered only, and then ten or twelve grains thereof make an amethyst color.

Wismut must be dissolved in aqua regis and precipitated with liquor of flints, and then sweetened and dried. Of this four or five grains turn an ounce of the mass into a sapphire color, but not so natural as gold does. Granite may be powder only, and then ten or fifteen grains thereof tinge an ounce of the mass into a fine green color not unlike to the natural smaragdine.

TO PROVE WHAT KIND OF METAL THERE IS IN ANY ORE ALTHOUGH YOU HAVE BUT A VERY FEW GRAINS THEREOF SO AS THAT YOU CANNOT MAKE PROOF THEREOF THE ORDINARY WAY WITH LEAD

Take two or four grains (if you have no greater quantity) of any ore that you have, and put it to half an ounce of Venice glass. Melt them together in a crucible (the crucible being covered) and according to the tincture that the glass receives from the ore, so may you judge what kind of metal there is in the ore. For if it be a copper ore, then the glass will be tinged with a sea-green colon
If copper and iron, a grass-green.
If iron, a dark yellow.
If tin, a pale yellow.
If silver, a whitish yellow.
If gold, a fine sky colon
If gold and silver together, a smaragdine colon
If gold, silver, copper, and iron together, an amethyst colon

A PRETTY OBSERVATION UPON THE MELTING OF COPPER AND TIN TOGETHER

First, make two bullets of red copper of the same magnitude. Make also two bullets of the purest tin in the same mold as the others were made. Weigh all four bullets and observe the weight well. Then melt the copper bullets first. Upon their being melted, put the two tin bullets and melt them together, but have a care that the tin fume not away. Then cast this molten mixture in the same molds as before, and it will scarce make three bullets, but yet they weigh as heavy as the four did before they were melted together.

I suppose the copper condenses the body of the tin which before was very porous, and which condensation rather adds than diminishes the weight thereof.

A REMARKABLE OBSERVATION UPON THE MELTING OF SALT ARMONIAC AND CALX VIVE TOGETHER

Take salt armoniac and calx vive, of each a like quantity, and mix and melt them together. Note that calx of itself will not melt in less than eight hours with the strongest fire that can be made, but being mixed with this salt melts in half an hour and less like a metal with an indifferent fire.

This mixture being thus melted becomes a hard stone, out of which you may strike fire as out of a flint which, if you dissolve again in water, you shall have the salt armoniac in the same quantity as before, but fixed. Note that hard things have their congelation from salt armoniac, as horns, bones, and such like, for little fixed salt can be extracted from them, only volatile and armoniac.

An ounce of any of these volatile salts (as of horns, bones, amber, and such like) reduced into an acid liquor by distillation, condenses and endures a pound of oily matter.

AN EASY AND CHEAP POWDER LIKE UNTO AURUM FULMINANS

Take of salt of tartar one part, salt petre three parts, sulphur a third part, and grind these well together and dry them. A few grains of this powder being fired will give as great a clap as a musket when it is discharged.

TO MAKE THE ANTIMONIAL CUP AND TO CAST DIVERSE FIGURES OF ANTIMONY

Take the best crude antimony, very well powdered, and nitre - of each a pound - and of crude tartar, finely powdered, two pounds. Mix them well together and put them into a crucible. Cover the crucible and melt them. The regulus will fall to the bottom and be like a melted metal. Then pour it forth into a brass mortar, being first smeared over with oil.

Or, take two parts of powdered antimony and four parts of powder of crude tartar. Melt these as aforesaid.

This regulus you may (when you have enough of it) melt again and cast it into what maids you please. You may either make cups or what pictures you please, and of what figures you please. You may cast it into forms of shillings or half crowns, either of which if you put into two or three ounces of wine in an earthen glazed vessel, or glass, and infuse in a moderate heat all night, you may have a liquor in the morning which will induce vomit. The dose is from two drams to two ounces and a half.

Note that in the wine you may put a little cinnamon to correct and give a more grateful relish to it.

It is the custom to fill the antimonial cup with wine and to put as much wine round about between that and the little earthen cup where it stands, and so infuse it all night, and then drink up all that wine. But I fear that so much wine will be too much as being three or four ounces, when as we seldom exceed the quantity of two ounces of the infusion of antimony.

These cups or pictures will last forever and be as effectual after a thousand times infusion as at first. And if they be broken at any time (as easily they may, being as brittle as glass) they may be cast again into what forms you please.

Note that he that casts them must be skillful in making his spawde, as also in scouring of them and making them bright afterwards, for if they be carefully handled they will look even as bright as silver.

BOOK VI

THE SPAGYRICAL ANATOMY OF GOLD AND SILVER TOGETHER WITH THE CURIOSITIES THEREIN AND CHIEFEST PREPARATIONS THEREOF

I shall first endeavor to show whence gold had its origin, and what the matter thereof is, as nature (says Sendivogius) is in the will of God, and God created her. So nature made for herself a seed, with her will in the elements. Now she indeed is one, yet she brings forth diverse things, but she operates nothing without a sperm. Whatsoever the sperm will, nature operates, for she is as it were the instrument of any artificers. The sperm therefore of everything is better and more profitable than nature herself. For you shall from nature do as much without a sperm as a goldsmith without fire or a husbandman without grain or feed. Now the sperm of anything is the elixir, the balsam of sulphur, and the same as humidum radicale is in metals. But to proceed to what concerns our purpose.

Four elements generate a sperm, by the will of God, and the imagination of nature. For, as the sperm of a man has its canter or the vessel of its seed in the kidneys, so the four elements by their indefinite motion (every one according to its quality) cast forth a sperm into the center of the earth where it is digested and by motion is sent abroad. Now the center of the earth is a certain empty place where nothing can rest. The four elements send forth their qualities into the circumference of the canter. As a male sends forth his seed into the womb of the female which, after it has received a due portion, casts out the rest, so it happens in the center of the earth that the magnetic power of a part of any place attracts something and the rest is cast forth into stones and other excrements. For something has its origin from this fountain, and there is nothing in the world produced but by this fountain. As for example, set upon an even table a vessel of water which may be placed in the middle thereof, and round about it set diverse things, and diverse colors, also salt, etc., everything by itself. Then pour the water into the middle, and you shall then see water to run every way, and when any stream touches the red color, it will be made red by it. If the water touches the salt, it will contract the taste of salt from it, and so of the rest. Now the water does not change the places, but the diversity of places changes the water. In like manner, the seed or sperm, being cast forth by the four elements from the canter of the earth unto the superficies thereof, passes through various places, and according to the nature of the place is anything produced. If it come to a pure place of earth and water, a pure thing is made.

The seed and sperm of all things is but one, and yet it generates diverse things, as it appears by the former example. The sperm while it is in the center is indifferent to all forms, but when it is come into any determinate place, it changes no more its form. The sperm while it is in the center can as easily produce a tree as a metal, and an herb as a stone, and one more precious than another according to the purity of the place. Now this sperm is produced of elements thus. These four are never quiet but, by reason of their contrariety, mutually act one upon another, and every one of itself sends forth its own subtlety, and they agree in the canter. Now in this canter is the Archaeus, the servant of nature which, mixing those sperms together, sends them abroad and by distillation sublimes them by the heat of a continual motion unto the superficies of the earth. For the earth is porous, and the vapor (or wind, as the philosophers call it) is by distilling through the pores of the earth resolved into water, of which all things are produced. Let therefore as I said before, all sons of Art, know that the sperm of metals is not different from the sperm of all things, being a humid vapor. Therefore, in vain do artists endeavor the reduction of metals into their first matter which is only a vapor. Now, says Bernard Trevisan, when philosophers speak of a first matter they did not mean this vapor, but the second matter which is an unctuous water which to us is the first, because we never find the former. Now the specification of this vapor into distinct metals is thus. This vapor passes in its distillation through the earth, through places either cold or hot. If through hot and pure, where the fatness of sulphur sticks to the sides thereof, then that vapor (which philosophers call the mercury of philosophers) mixes, and joins itself unto that fatness which afterwards it sublimes with itself. Then it becomes, leaving the name of a vapor, an unctuosity, which afterwards coming by sublimation into other places (which the antecedent vapor did purge) where the earth is subtle, pure, and humid, fills the pores thereof and is joined to it, and so it becomes gold. Where it is hot and something impure, it becomes silver. But if that fatness comes to impure places which are cold, it is made lead. If that place be pure and mixed with sulphur, it becomes copper. For by how much the more pure and warm the place is, so much the more excellent does it make the metals. Now this first matter of metals is a humid, viscous, incombustible, subtle substance, incorporated with an earth subtlety, being equally and strongly mixed per minima in the caverns of the earth. But, as in many things, there is a twofold unctuosity (whereof one is, as it were, internal, retained in the canter of the thing lest it should be destroyed by fire which cannot be without the destruction of the substance itself wherein it is; the other is, as it were, external, feculent, and combustible). So in all metals except gold, there is a twofold unctuosity. One is external, sulphurous, and inflammable which is joined to it by accident and does not belong to the total union with the terrestrial parts of the thing. The other is internal, very subtle, and incombustible, because it is of the substantial composition of argent vive and, therefore, cannot be destroyed by fire, unless with the destruction of the whole substance, whence it appears what the cause is that metals are more or less durable in the fire. For those which abound with that internal unctuosity are less consumed, as it appears in silver and, especially, in gold. Hence, Rosarius says the philosophers could never by any means find out anything that could endure the fire, but that unctuous humidity only which is perfect and incombustible. Geber also asserts the same when he says that imperfect bodies have superfluous humidities and sulphureity generating a combustible blackness in them, and corrupting them. They have also an impure, feculent, and combustible terrestriety so gross as that it hinders ingression and fusion. But a perfect metal as gold, has neither this sulphurous nonterrestrial impurity, I mean, when it is fully maturated and melted. For while it is in concoction it has both joined to it, as you may see in the golden ore, but then they do not adhere to it so, but that it may be purified from them which other metals cannot, but are both destroyed together if you attempt to separate the one from the other. Besides gold has so little of these corruptible principles mixed with it that the inward sulphur or metalline spirit does sometimes and in some places overcome them of itself, as we may see in the gold which is found very pure sometimes in the superficies of the earth and in the sea sands, and is many times as pure as any refined gold.

Now, this gold which is found in sands and rivers is not generated there, as says Gregorius Agricola in his third book, De Re Metallica, but is washed down from the mountains with fountains that run from thence.

There is also a flaming gold found (as Paracelsus says) in the tops of mountains which is indeed separated of itself from all impurities and is as pure as any refined gold whatsoever. So that you see, that gold, although it had an extrinsical sulphur and earth mixed with it, yet it is sometimes separated from it of itself, viz., by that fiery spirit that is in it. Now this pure gold (as says Sendivogius) nature would have perfected into an elixir, but was hindered by the crude air, which crude air is indeed nothing else than that extrinsical sulphur which it meets with and is joined to in the earth, and which fills with its violence the pores thereof, and hinders the activity thereof. This is that prison which the sulphur (as says the aforesaid author) is locked up in so that it cannot act upon its body, viz., mercury and concoct it into the seed of gold, as otherwise it would do. This is that dark body (as says Penotus) that is interposed between the philosophical sun and moon and keeps off the influences of the one from the other. Now if any skillful philosopher could wittily separate this adventitious impurity from gold while it is yet living, he would set sulphur at liberty, and for this his service he should be gratified with three kingdoms, viz., vegetable, animal, and mineral. I mean he could remove that great obstruction which hinders gold from being digested into the elixir. For, as says Sendivogius, the elixir or tincture of philosophers is nothing else but gold digested into the highest degree. For the gold of the vulgar is as an herb without seed, but when living gold (for common gold never can by reason that the spirits are bound up and, indeed, as good as dead and not possibly to be reduced to that activity which is required for the producing of the sperm of gold) is ripened it gives a seed which multiplies even ad infinitum. Now the reason of this barrenness of gold that it produces not a seed, is the aforesaid crude air, viz., impurities. You may see this illustrated by this example.

We see that orange trees in Polonia do grow like other trees, also in Italy and elsewhere, where their native soil is, and yield fruit, because they have sufficient heat. But in these colder countries they are barren and never yield any fruit, because they are oppressed with cold. If at any time nature be wittily and sweetly helped, then art can perfect what nature could not. After the same manner it is in metals, for gold would yield fruit and seed in which it might multiply itself, if it were helped by the industry of the skillful artist who knows how to promote nature and to separate these sulphurous and earthly impurities from gold. For there is a sufficient heat in living gold which if it were stirred up by extrinsical heat, to digest it into a seed. By extrinsical heat I do not mean the heat of the celestial sun, but that heat which is in the earth and stirs up the seed, the living spirit that is in all subterranean sperms to multiply and, indeed, makes gold become gold.

Now this is a heat of putrefaction occasioned by acid spirits in the earth fermenting, as you may see by this example related by Albertus Magnus, but to which the reason was given by Sendivogius. There was, says the former author, certain grains of gold found between the teeth of a dead man in the grave, wherefore he conceived there was a power in the body of man to make and fix gold. But the reason is far otherwise, as says the latter author. He says argent vive was by some physician conveyed into the body of this man when he was alive, either by unction or by turbith, or some such as was the custom. It is the nature of mercury to ascend to the mouth of the patient and through the excoriation of the mouth to be avoided with the phlegm. Now, then, if in such a cure the sick man died, that mercury not having passage out remained between the teeth in the mouth. That carcass became the natural vessel of mercury, and so for a long time being shut up, was congealed by its proper sulphur into gold by the natural heat of putrefaction, being purified by the corrosive phlegm of the carcass, but if the mineral mercury had not been brought in thither, gold had never been produced there. This is a most true example that as mercury is by the proper sulphur that is in itself, being stirred up and helped by an extrinsical heat, coagulated into gold, unless it be hindered by any accident, or have not a requisite extrinsical heat, or a convenient place, so also nature does in the bowels of earth produce of mercury only gold and silver, and other metals according to the disposition of the place and matrix, which assertion is further cleared by the rule of reduction. For if it be true that all things consist of that which they may be reduced into, then gold consists of mercury, because (as most grant, Paracelsus affirms, and many at this day profess they can do) it may be reduced into it.

There is a way by which the tincture of gold which is the soul thereof, and fixes it, may be so fully extracted that the remaining substance will be sublimed like arsenic and may be as easily reduced into mercury as sublimate. If so, and if all mercury may be reduced into a transparent water, as it may (according to the process set down earlier, and as I know how another better and easier way to turn a pound of mercury of itself into a clear water in half an hour, which is one of the greatest secrets I know or care to know, together with what may be produced thence, and shall crave leave to be silent in) may not that water in some sense, if it be well rectified, be called a kind of living gold out of which you may perhaps make a medicine and a menstruum unfit for the vulgar to know.

It appears now from what is premised that the immediate matter of gold is probably mercury, and not certain salts and I know not what as many dream of, and that the extrinsical heat is from within the earth and not the heat of the sun, as some imagine (because in the hottest countries there is all or almost all gold generated) who if they considered that in cold countries also are and, as in Scotland were gold mines in King James' time, would be of another mind than to think that the celestial sun could penetrate so as to heat the earth so deep as most gold lies.

I now having in some measure discovered what the intrinsical and extrinsical heat and the matter of gold is, I shall next endeavor to explain what those three principles are, viz., salt, sulphur, and mercury, of which argent vive and gold consist. Know therefore that after nature had received from the most High God the privilege of all things upon the monarchy of this world, she began to distribute places and provinces to every thing according to its dignity, and in the first place did constitute the four elements to be the princes of the world and, that the will of the Most High (in whose will nature in placed) might be fulfilled, ordained that they should act upon one another incessantly. The fire therefore began to act upon the air and produced sulphur. The air also began to act upon the water and produced mercury. The water also began to act upon the earth and produced salt. Now the earth not having whereon to act produced nothing, but became the subject of what was produced. So then there were produced three principles, but our ancient philosophers, not so strictly considering the matter, described only two acts of the elements and so named but two principles, viz., sulphur and mercury, or else they were willing to be silent in the other, speaking only to the sons of art.
The sulphur, therefore, of philosophers (which indeed is the sulphur of metals and of all things) is not, as many think, that common combustible sulphur which is sold in shops, but is another thing far differing from that, and is combustible, not burning nor heating, but preserving and restoring all things which it is in. It is the calidum innatum of everything, the fire of nature, the created light, and of the

nature of the sun, and is called the sun. Thus whatsoever in anything is fiery and airy is sulphur, not that anything is wholly sulphurous, but what in it is most thin and subtle, having the essence of the natural fire and the nature of the created light which indeed is that sulphur which wise philosophers have in all ages with great diligence endeavored to extract, and with its proper mercury to fix, and so to perfect the great magistery of nature. Now of all things in the world there is nothing that has more of this sulphur in it than gold and silver, but especially gold, insomuch that oftentimes it is called sulphur because sulphur is the most predominant and excellent principle in it, and being in it more than in all things besides.

Mercury is not here taken for common argent vive, but it is the humidum radicals of everything, that pure aqueous, unctuous, and viscous humidity of the matter. It is of the nature of the moon and it is called the moon and for this reason, viz., because it is humid, as also because it is capable of receiving the influence and light of the sun, viz., sulphur. Salt is that fixed permanent earth which is the center of everything that is incorruptible and unalterable, and it is the supporter and nurse of the humidum radicale with which it is strongly mixed. Now this salt has in it a seed, viz., its galidum innatum which is sulphur and its humidum radicale, which is mercury, and yet these three are not distinct or to be separated, but are one homogenous thing, having upon a different account diverse names. For in respect of its heat and fiery substance, it is called sulphur. In respect of its humidity it is called mercury, and in respect of its terrestrial siccity it is called salt, all which are in gold perfectly united, depurated, and fixed.

Gold therefore is the most noble and solid of all metals, of a yellow colon, compacted of principles digested to the utmost height and, therefore fixed.

Silver is in the next place of dignity to gold and differs from it in digestion chiefly. I said chiefly, because there is some small impurity besides adhering to silver.

Now, having given some small account of the original matter first, and second of the manner of the growth of gold, I shall in the next place set down some curiosities therein and preparation thereof. The preparations are chiefly three, viz., aurum potabile which is the mixtion thereof with other liquors; oil of gold which is gold liquid by itself without the mixture of any other liquor; and the tincture which is the extraction of the color thereof.

DR. ANTHONY'S FAMOUS AURUM POTABILE AND OIL OF GOLD

Dissolve pure fine gold in aqua regis according to art (the aqua regis being made of a pound of aqua fortis and four ounces of salt armoniac distilled together by retort in sand) which clear solution put into a large glass of a wide neck and upon it pour drop by drop oil of tartar made per deliquium, until the aqua aegis which before was yellow becomes clear and white, for that is a sign that all calx of gold is settled to the bottom. Then let it stand all night, and in the morning pour off the clear liquor, and wash the calx four or five times with common spring water, being warmed, and dry it with a most gentle heat.

Note, and that well, that if the heat be too great, the calx takes fire presently like gun powder and flies away to your danger and loss. Therefore, it is best to dry it in the sun, or on a stone, stirring it diligently with a wooden spatule. To this calx add half a part of the powder of sulphur. Mix them together, and in an open crucible let the sulphur burn away in the fire, putting a gentle fire to it at the first, and in the end a most strong fire for the space of an hour so that the calx may in some manner be reverberated and become most subtle, which keep in a vial close stopped for your use.

Then make a spirit of urine after this manner. Take the urine of a healthy man drinking wine moderately. Put it into a gourd which you must stop close, and set in horse dung for the space of forty days. Then distill it by alembic in sand into a large receiver until all the humidity be distilled off. Rectify this spirit by cohobation three times so that the spirit only may rise. Then distill it in sand by a glass with a long neck having a large receiver annexed and closed very well to it, and the spirit will be elevated into the top of the vessel like crystal without any aqueous humidity accompanying of it. Let this distillation be continued until all the spirits be risen. These crystals must be dissolved in distilled rain water and be distilled as before. This must be done six times and every time you must take fresh rain water distilled. Then put these crystals into a glass bolt head, close hermetically, and set in the moderate heat of a balneum for the space of fifteen days so that they may be reduced into a most clear liquor. To this liquor add an equal weight of spirit of wine, very well rectified, and let them be digested in balneum the space of twelve days, in which time they will be united. Then take the calx of gold above said, and pour upon it of these united spirits as much as will cover them three fingers breadth. Digest them in a gentle heat until the liquor be tinged as red as blood. Decant off the tincture and put on more of the aforesaid spirits and do as before until all the tincture be extracted. Then put all the tincted spirits together and digest them ten or twelve days, after which time abstract the spirit with a gentle heat and cohobate it once. And then the calx will remain in the bottom like an oil as red as blood and of a pleasant odor, and which will be dissolved in any liquor. Wherefore this oil may be the succedaneum of true gold. If you distill the same solution by retort in sand there will come over after the first part of the menstruum the tincture with the other part thereof, as red as blood, the earth which is left in the bottom of the vessel being black, dry, spongy, and light. The menstruum must be vapored away and the oil of gold will remain by itself, which must be kept as a great treasure. And this is Dr. Anthony's Aurum Potabile.

Four or eight grains of this oil taken in what manner soever wonderfully refreshes the spirits, and works several ways, especially by sweat.

THE TRUE OIL OF GOLD

Take an ounce of leaf gold and dissolve it in four ounces of the rectified water of mercury. Digest them in horse dung the space of two months. Then evaporate the mercurial water, and at the bottom you shall have the true oil of gold which is radically dissolved.

A TINCTURE OF GOLD

Dissolve pure gold in aqua regis. Precipitate it with the oil of sand into a yellow powder which you must dulcify with warm water, and then dry it (this will not be fired as aurum fulminans). This powder is twice as heavy as the gold that was put in, the cause of which is the salt of the flints precipitating itself with the gold. Put this yellow powder into a crucible and make it glow a little, and it will be turned into the highest and fairest purple that ever you saw, but if it stands longer it will be brown. Then pour upon it the strongest spirit of salt (for it will dissolve it better than any aqua regis) on which dissolution pour on the best rectified spirit of wine, and digest them together. By a long digestion some part of the gold will fall to the bottom like a white snow and may with borax, tartar, and salt nitre be melted into a white metal as heavy as gold and, afterwards with antimony, may recover its yellow color again. Then evaporate the spirit of salt and of wine, and the gold tincture remains at the bottom and is of great virtue.

ANOTHER TINCTURE OF GOLD

Take of the aforesaid yellow calx of gold precipitated with oil of sand, one part, and three or four parts of the liquor of sand or of crystals. Mix them well together and put them into a crucible in a gentle heat at first, so that the moisture of the oil may vapor away (which it will not do easily because of the dryness of the sand which retains the moisture thereof, so that it flies away like molten alum or borax). When no more will vapor away, increase your fire until the crucible be red hot and the mixture ceases bubbling. Then put it into a wind furnace and cover it so that no ashes fall into it. Make a strong fire about it for the space of an hour, and the mixture will be turned into a transparent ruby. Then take it out, beat it, and extract the tincture with spirit of wine which will become like thin blood, and that which remains undissolved may be melted into a white metal as the former.

ANOTHER TINCTURE OF GOLD

Hang plates of gold over the fume of argent vive, and they will become white, friable, and fluxile as wax. This is called the magnesia of gold, as says Paracelsus, in finding out of which (says he) philosophers as Thomas Aquinas and Rupescissa with their followers took a great deal of pains, but in vain, and it is a memorable secret and indeed very singular for melting of metals that are not easily fluxible. Now, then, gold being thus prepared and melted together with the mercury, is become a brittle substance which must be powdered and out of it a tincture may be drawn for the transmuting of metals.

ANOTHER TINCTURE

Take half an ounce of pure gold and dissolve it in aqua regis. Precipitate it with oil of flints, dulcify the calx with warm water and dry it, and so it is prepared for your work. Then take regulus martis powdered and mix it with three parts of salt nitre, both which put into a crucible and make them glow gently at first. Then give a strong melting fire and then this mixture will become to be of a purple colon, which then take out and beat to powder. Add to three parts of this one part of the calx of gold prepared as before. Put them into a wind furnace in a strong crucible, and make them melt as a metal. So will the nitrum antimoniatum in the melting take the calx of gold to itself and dissolve it, and the mixture will come to be of an amethyst colon Let this stand flowing in the fire until the whole mass be as transparent as a rubine which you may try by taking a little out and cooling of it. If the mixture does not flow well, cast in some more salt nitre. When it is completely done, cast it forth being flowing into a brazen mortar and it will be like an oriental rubine. Then powder it before it be cold. Then put it into a vial and with the spirit of wine extract the tincture.
This is one of the best preparations of gold and of most excellent use in medicine.

ANOTHER TINCTURE

First make a furnace fit for the purpose which must be closed at the top and have a pipe to which a recipient with a flat bottom must be fitted. When this furnace is thus fitted, put in three or four grains, not above at once, of aurum fulminans which, as soon as the furnace is hot, flies away into the recipient through the pipe like a purple colored fume and is turned into a purple colored powder. Then put in three or four grains more and do as before until you have enough flowers of gold (that which fly not away but remain at the bottom, may with borax be melted into good gold). Then take them out and pour upon them rectified spirit of wine tartarized, and digest them in ashes until the spirit be colored blood red which you must them evaporate and at the bottom will be a blood red tincture of no small virtue.

AURUM FULMINANS

Take the purest gold you can get and pour on it four times as much aqua regia. Stop your glass with a paper, and set it in warm ashes. So will the aqua regia in an hour or two take up the gold and become a yellow water, if it be strong enough. (Be sure that your gold has no copper in it, for then your labor will be lost, because the copper will be precipitated with the gold and hinder the firing thereof). Then pour on this yellow water drop by drop pure oil of tartar made per deliquium, so will the gold be precipitated into a dark yellow powder and the water be clear. Note that you pour not on more oil of tartar than is sufficient for the precipitation, otherwise it will dissolve part of the precipitated gold to your prejudice. Pour off the clear liquor by inclination, and dulcify the calx with distilled rain water warmed. Then set this calx in the sun or some warm place to dry, take great heed and especial care that you set it not in a place too hot, for it will presently take fire and fly away like thunder and not without great danger to the standers by, if the quantity be great. This is the common way to make aurum fulminaris, and has considerable difficulties in the preparation. But the best way is to precipitate gold dissolved in aqua regis by the spirit of salt armoniac or of urine, for by this way the gold is made purer than by the other and gives a far greater crack and sound. Note that the salt of the spirits which is precipitated with the gold must be washed away and the gold dulcified as before.

A few grains of this being fired give a crack and sound as great as a musket when it is discharged and will blow up anything more forcibly far than gunpowder, and it is a powder that will quickly and easily be fired.

This is of use for physick as it is in powder, but especially it is used in making the foregoing tincture.

TO MAKE GOLD GROW IN A GLASS LIKE A TREE WHICH IS CALLED THE GOLDEN TREE OF THE PHILOSOPHERS

Take oil of sand, as much as you please, and pour upon it the same quantity of oil of tartar per deliquium. Shake them well together so that they be incorporated and become as one liquor of a thin consistency.

Then is your menstruum or liquor prepared. Then dissolve gold in aqua regia, and evaporate the menstruum and dry the calx in the fire, but make it not too hot, for it will thereby lose its growing quality. Then take it out and break it into little bits, not into powder. Put those bits into the aforesaid liquor (that they may lay a finger's breadth the one from the other) in a very clear glass. Keep the liquor from the air, and you shall see that those bits of the calx will presently begin to grow. First they will swell. Then they will put forth one or two stems, and then diverse branches and twigs so exactly as that you cannot choose but exceedingly to wonder. This growing is real and not imaginary only. Note that the glass must stand still and not be moved.

ANOTHER WAY

Calcine fine gold in aqua regia so that it becomes a calx, which put into a gourd glass, and pour upon it good and fresh aqua regia and the water of gradation, so that they cover the calx four finger's breadth. This menstruum abstract in the third degree of fire until no more will ascend. This distilled water pour on it again and abstract it as before, and this do so often until you see the gold rise in the glass and grow in the form of a tree having many boughs and leaves.

TO MAKE GOLD GROW AND BE INCREASED IN THE EARTH

Take leaves of gold and bury them in the earth which looks towards the east. Let it often be soiled with man's urine and dove's dung, and you shall see that in a short time they will be increased.

The reason of this growth, I conceive, may be the gold's attracting that universal vapor and sperm that comes from the canter through the earth (as has been spoken in the Anatomy of Gold) and by the heat of putrefaction of the dung putrifying and assimilating it to itself.

A REMARKABLE OBSERVATION UPON A GOLDEN MARCASITE

There is found a certain stone in Bononia, which some call a golden marcasite, some a salary magnes, that receives light from the sun in the daytime and gives it forth in the dark.

About this there has been much reasoning among philosophers, as whether light be really a body, or any kind of substance, or an accident only, and whether this stone had any gold in it or no, and what it did consist of. He that first discovered it thought that he had found a thing that would transmute metals into gold (by which it appears that there seemed to be something of gold in it or something more glorious than gold). But his hopes were frustrated by a fruitless labor, notwithstanding which I conceive there might be some immature or crude gold in it; for crude gold is a subject (being there is some life in it) that is most fit to receive the influences of the sun according to the unanimous consent of all philosophers and, therefore, is by them not only called salary, but sol, the sun itself.

It is prepared for the receiving of light thus. It is calcined two ways. First it is brought into a most subtle powder with a very strong fire in a crucible. Secondly, being thus brought into a powder, it is made up into cakes as big as a dollar or a piece-of-eight, either with common water alone or with the white of an egg. Put those cakes being dried by themselves into a wind furnace S S S with coals and calcine them in a most strong fire for the space of four or five hours. When the furnace is cold, take them out, and if they be not sufficiently calcined the first time (which is known by their giving but little light) then reiterate the calcination after the same manner as before, which is sometimes to be done thrice. That is the best which is made with the choicest stones that are clean, pure, and diaphanous, and gives the best light. With this being powdered, you may make the forms of diverse animals, of what shapes you please, which you must keep in boxes, and they will, receiving light from the sun in the daytime, give light in the night or in a dark place which light will vanish by degrees.

THE VIRTUES OF THE AFORESAID PREPARATIONS OF GOLD

With the aforesaid preparations, the ancients did not only preserve the health and strength of their bodies, but also prolong their lives to a very old age, and not that only, but cured thoroughly the epilepsy, apoplexy, elephantiasis, leprosy, melancholy, madness, the quartain, the gout, dropsy, plurisy, all manner of fevers, the jaundice, lucs venerea, the wolfe, cancer, nolli nes angere, asthma, consumption, the stone, stopping of the urine, inward impostumes, and such like diseases which most men account incurable. For there is such a potent fire lying in prepared gold which does not only consume deadly humors, but also renews the very marrow of the bones, and raises up the whole body of man being half dead.

They that use any of these preparations for any of the foregoing diseases must take themselves to their bed for the space of two or three hours and expect sweating to ensue for, indeed, it will send forth sweat plentifully and with ease, and leave no impurity or superfluity in the whole body. Note that they must take it fourteen days together in appropriate liquors.

Let young men that expect long life take any of the aforesaid preparations once in a month, and in the morning, but they must abstain from neat and drink until the evening of the same day, for in that time that matter will be digested into the radical humor, whereby the strength of the body is wonderfully increased, beauty does flourish most wonderfully, and continues until extreme old age.

Let old men take it twice in a month, for by this means will their old age be fresh until the appointed time of death.

Let young women and maids take it once in a month after their menstrua, for by this means they will look fresh and beautiful.
Let women that are in travail take it, and it will help and strengthen them to bring forth without much pain, notwithstanding many difficulties.

Let it be given to women that have passed the years of their menstrua once or twice a month, and it will preserve them very fresh, and many times cause their menstrua to return and make them capable again of bearing children.

It cures the plague and expells the matter of a carbuncle by sweat most potently.

When I say that this, or it will do thus or thus, I mean any one of the forementioned preparations, viz., aurum potabile, oils or tincture of gold.

THE PREPARATIONS OF SILVER IN GENERAL

All the several preparations of gold may, except that of aurum fulminans, be applied to silver, of which being thus prepared the virtues are inferior to those of gold, yet come nearer to them than those of any other matter whatsoever, or howsoever prepared.

Note that silver has some peculiar preparations which neither gold nor any other metals are capable of.

A GREEN TINCTURE OF SILVER

Take fine silver and dissolve it in twice so much rectified spirit of nitre. Then abstract half of the said spirit in sand. Let it stand a day or two in a cold place, and much of the silver will shoot into crystals, and in oft doing, most of it.

These crystals are very bitter, yet may be made into pills and taken inwardly from three grains to twelve. They purge very securely and gently, and color the lips, tongue, and mouth black. If in this dissolution of silver before it be brought to crystals, half so much mercury be dissolved and both shoot together into crystals, you shall have a stone not much unlike to alum. This purges sooner and better, and is not so bitter. It colons the nails, hair, skin, if it be dissolved in rainwater, with a lovely brown, red, or black, according as you put more or less thereof.

Take of the aforesaid crystals of silver and mix with them a like quantity of pure saltpetre well powdered. Then put this mixture into the distilling vessel at the bottom of which must be powdered coals to the thickness of two fingers breadth. Then make a strong fire so that the vessel and coals be red hot. Put in a dram of the aforesaid mixture, and it will presently sublime in a silver fume into the recipient which, being settled, put in more and do so until you have enough. Take out the flowers and digest them in the best alcholizated spirit of wine so that thereby the tincture may be extracted which will be green.

A GREEN OIL OF SILVER

Take of the abovesaid crystals of silver one part, of spirit of salt armoniac two or three parts, and digest them together in a glass with a long neck, well stopped, twelve or fourteen days. So will the spirit of salt armoniac be colored with a very specious blue color. Pour it off and filter it. Then put it into a small retort and draw off most of the spirit of ammoniac, and there will remain in the bottom a grass green liquor. Then draw off all the spirit, and there will remain in the bottom a salt which may be purified with spirit of wine or be put into a retort. Then there will distill off a subtle spirit and a sharp oil.

This green liquor is of great use for the gilding of all things presently. If you take common rainwater distilled, and dissolve and digest the aforesaid crystals of silver for a few days, you shall after the appearance of diverse colors find an essence at the bottom, not so bitter as the former, but sweet. In this liquor may all metals in a gentle heat by long digestion be maturated and made fit for medicine. But note that they must first be reduced into salts, for then they are no more dead bodies, but by this preparation have obtained a new life, and are the metals of the philosophers.

TO MAKE OIL OF SILVER PER DELIQUIUM

Take of the aforesaid salts or crystals of silver and reverberate them in a very gentle fire. Then put them into a cellar on a marble stone, and they will in two months time be resolved into a liquor.

TO MAKE A LIQUOR OF SILVER THAT SHALL MAKE THE GLASS WHEREIN IT IS SO EXCEEDING COLD THAT NO MAN IS ABLE FOR THE COLDNESS THEREOF TO HOLD IT IN HIS HAND ANY LONG TIME

Take the aforesaid salt of silver, pour upon it the spirit of salt armoniac, dissolve it thoroughly, and it will do as abovesaid.

With a glass being full of this liquor you may condense the air into water in the heat of the summer, as also freeze water.

TO MAKE SILVER AS WHITE AS SNOW

Take of the calx of silver made by dissolution of it in aqua fortis. Dulcify it, boil it in a lixivium made of soap ashes, and it will be white as any snow.

TO MAKE THE SILVER TREE OF THE PHILOSOPHERS

Take four ounces of aqua fortis in which dissolve an ounce of fine silver. Then take two ounces of aqua fortis in which is dissolved half an ounce of argent vive. Mix these two liquors together in a clear glass with a pint of pure water. Stop the glass very close and you shall see day after day a tree to grow by little and little which is wonderful pleasant to behold.

I have set down several vulgar preparations of gold and silver, and of almost all things else, I shall now crave leave to give an account of some philosophical preparations of the philosophers gold and silver. For indeed the art of preparing them is the true alchemy, in comparison of which all the chemical discoveries are but abortives and found out by accident, viz., by endeavoring after this. I would not have the world believe that I pretend to the understanding of them. Yet I would have them know that I am not incredulous as touching the possibility of that great philosophical work which many have so much labored after and may have found. To me there is nothing in the world seems more possible, and whosoever shall without prejudice read over the book entitled The New Light Of Alchemy shall almost whether he will or not (unless he resolves not to believe anything though never so credible) be convinced of the possibility of it. What unworthiness God saw in gold more than in other things that he should deny the seed of multiplication (which is the perfection of the creatures) to it, and give it to all things besides, seems to me to be a question as hard to be resolved, yea, and harder than the finding out the elixir itself, in the discovering of which the greatest difficulty is, not to be convinced of the easiness thereof. If the preparations were difficult many more would find it out than do (says Sendivogius) for they cast themselves upon most difficult operations and are very subtle in difficult discoveries which the philosophers never dreamed of. Nay, says the aforenamed author, if Hermes himself were now living together with subtle witted Geber and most profound Raimund Lullie, they would be accounted by our chemists not for philosophers, but rather for learners. They were ignorant of those so many distillations, so many circulations, so many calcinations, and so many other innumerable operations of artists nowadays used which, indeed, men of this age did find out and invented out of their books. Yet there is one thing wanting to us which they did, viz., to know how to make the Philosophers Stone, or physical tincture the processes of which according to some philosophers are these.

THE PROCESS OF THE ELIXIR ACCORDING TO PARACELSUS

Take the mineral electrum, being immature and made very subtle. Put it into its own sphere so that the impurities and superfluities may be washed away. Then purge it as much as possibly you can with stibium after the alchemystical way, lest by its impurity you suffer prejudice. Then resolve it in the stomach of an estridge which is brought forth in the earth and through the sharpness of the eagle is comforted in its virtue.

Now when the electrum is consumed, and has after its solution received the color of a marigold, do not forget to reduce it into a spiritual transparent essence which is like to true amber. Then add half so much, as the electrum did weigh before its preparation, of the extended eagle, and oftentimes abstract from it the stomach of the estridge, and by this means the electrum will be made more spiritual. Now when the stomach of the estridge is wearied with labor, it will be necessary to refresh it and always to abstract it. Lastly, when it has again lost its sharpness, add the tartarized quintessence, yet so that it be spoiled of its redness the height of four fingers and that pass over with it. This do so often until it be of itself white, and when it is enough and you see that sign, sublime it. So will the electrum be converted into the whiteness of an exalted eagle, and with a little more labor be transmuted into deep redness, and then it is fit for medicine.

THE PROCESS OF THE ELIXIR ACCORDING TO DIVI LESCHI GENUS AMO

Take of our earth through eleven degrees, eleven grains, of our gold, and not of the vulgar, one grain, of our tuna, not of the vulgar, grains two. But be you admonished that you take not the gold and silver of the vulgar, for they are dead, but take ours which are living. Then put them into our fire, and there will thence be made a dry liquor. First the earth will be resolved into water which is called the mercury of philosophers, and in that water it will resolve the bodies of the sun and moon and consume them so that there remain but the tenth part with one part, and this will be the humidum radicale metallicum. Then take the water of the salt nitre of our earth, in which there is a living stream if you digest the pit knee deep. Take therefore the water of it, but take it clear and set over it that humidum radicals, and put it over the fire of putrefaction, but not so much as was that in the first operation. Govern all things with a great deal of discretion until there appear colors like to the tail of a peacock. Govern it by digesting of it, and be not weary until these colons cease and there appear throughout the whole a green color, and so of the rest, and when you shall see in the bottom ashes of a fiery color and the water almost red, open the vessel, dip in a feather, and smear over some iron with it. If it tinge, have in readiness that water which is the menstruum of the world (out of the sphere of the moon so often rectified until it can calcine gold). Put in so much of that water as was the cold air which went in. Boil it again with the former fire until it tinge again.

THE PROCESS OF THE PHILOSOPHERS STONE ACCORDING TO PONTANUS

Take the matter and grind it with a physical contrition as diligently as may be. Then set it upon the fire and let the proportion of fire be known, viz., that it only stir up the matter, and in a short time that fire without any other laying on of hands will accomplish the whole work, because it will putrefy, corrupt, generate, and perfect, and make to appear the three principal colors: black, white, and red. And by the means of our fire, the medicine will be multiplied if it be joined with the crude matter, not only in quantity but also in virtue. Withall, they might therefore search out this fire (which is mineral, equal, continual, vapors not away, except it be too much stirred up; partakes of sulphur, is taken from elsewhere than from the matter; pulls down all things, dissolves, congeals, and calcines, and is artificial to find out, and that by a compendious and near way without any cost, at least very small, is not transmuted with the matter because it is not of the matter). And you shall attain your wish, because it does the whole work, and is the key of the philosophers which they never revealed.

THE SMARAGDINE TABLE OF HERMES FROM WHENCE ALL ALCHEMY DID ARISE

True, without all falsity, certain and most true. That which is inferior is as that which is superior, and that which is superior is as that which is inferior, for the accomplishing of the miracles of one thing. And as all things were from one, by the mediation of one, so all things have proceeded from this one thing by adaptation. The Father thereof is the sun, and the Mother thereof the moon. The wind carried it in its belly. The nurse thereof is the earth.

The father of all the perfection of the whole world is this. The virtue thereof is entire, if it be turned into earth. Thou shalt separate the earth from the fire, the subtle from the thick, sweetly, with a great deal of judgment. It ascends from the earth up to heaven, and again descends down to the earth, and receives the powers of superiors and inferiors. So you have the glory of the whole world. Therefore let all obscurity fly from you. This is the strong fortitude of the whole fortitude, because it shall overcome everything that is subtle and penetrate every solid thing, as the world is created. Hence shall wonderful adaptations be, whereof this is the manner, wherefore I am called Hermes Trismegistus, having three parts of the philosophy of the whole world.
It is complete, what I have spoken of the operation of the sun.

POSTSCRIPT

If I shall hereafter see that what I have here done shall deserve a second edition, I shall "hereunto add some other parts of chemistry, viz., sublimation and calcination which here I have omitted (except what I have written by the way of reference to the perfecting of any kind of distillation). For indeed distillation (which is the making, extracting, or purifying of liquors) is the chiefest subject of this discourse and, indeed, the whole, except some spagyrical experiments and curiosities set down in the fifth book.